POWERFUL tips
for POWERFUL
teachers
Helping Youth Find Their Spiritual Wings

C.S. Bezas

ROSEHAVEN
PUBLISHING & DISTRIBUTION, INC.
Pleasant Grove, UT

Rosehaven Publishing & Distribution, Inc.
P.O. Box 247
Pleasant Grove, UT 84062
www.rosehavenpublishing.com

ISBN: 978-1-931858-11-3

Printed in the United States of America
09 08 07 06   10 9 8 7 6 5 4 3 2 1

Cover Design by Lori Nawyn

Internal design and layout by Professional Pre-Press, Pleasant Grove, UT

Powerful Tips for Powerful Teachers

Helping Youth Find Their Spiritual Wings

This book is dedicated to parents, leaders,
and teachers of youth throughout the world,
who dedicate their lives, their hearts, and their time
to the Lord's future leaders.

ACKNOWLEDGMENTS

I gratefully acknowledge publisher and editor Karlene Browning and her entire staff at Rosehaven Publishing for their stellar work on behalf of this book. I appreciate their vision of bringing forth books and products that bless the lives of others.

Lori Nawyn is to be commended as always for the beauty of her graphic design and the sweetness of her soul.

I thank Terrie Bittner for the strength of her teaching ability and her gift of insight with students. I am in awe of her gifts and have been inspired by them.

There have been numerous individuals throughout the years who have blessed my life with their inspired trainings and teacher in-service meetings. May the Lord greatly bless them for their quiet service.

My husband and children sacrificed kindly while I wrote this book. They more than deserve a bounty of hugs and time spent "with Mommy" – both now and for all eternity.

TABLE OF CONTENTS

List of 100 Scripture Mastery Verses can be found on page 122.

The gospel teacher's promise:

Nevertheless, ye are blessed,
for the testimony which ye have borne
is recorded in heaven for the angels
to look upon; and they rejoice over you,
and your sins are forgiven you.
(D&C 62:3)

Introduction

What an exciting thing to be asked to teach the gospel to the Lord's future leaders. These youth who sometimes squirm, burp, or sleep in our gospel classes will one day fill important leadership positions for the Church and kingdom of God. Each day we spend with them in the classroom or in our homes makes a difference in preparation for these tremendous roles.

Yet knowing this as a teacher is one thing; living it can be a difficult experience. Being mortal, we sometimes struggle with the day-to-day challenges of dealing with youth. Some days they're moody, sometimes they're bright. Some days they're selfish, some moments they are magnificently kind.

This book is intended to be a guide and comfort to you during the more difficult moments of your Christ-like tenure as a teacher, youth leader or parent of teens. Come back to this book time and again when you are in need of encouragement. Take time weekly to select a topic and reflect on it, then answer the questions contained within that topic's chapter. Record your thoughts in your own teaching journal. Not only will the record you create infuse you with strength for future times of fatigue or discouragement, but your written words of personal insights and problem-solving solutions will also inspire your family and future posterity. For was it not in this pattern that Nephi himself created the record we know and quote so well?

Nephi studied the scriptures. He loved the scriptures. He even quoted them within his record or journal. We can do the same. To teach the gospel of Jesus Christ effectively, no matter what group we're teaching, we must spend time immersed in the scriptures. We must ponder and develop our thoughts, finding ways to effectively present scriptural truths—all surrounded and influenced by the Spirit. The scriptures are to be our main text as we work with our youth. In fact, we have been asked to use only the scriptures and church-approved curriculum in our classrooms. This is for a wise purpose: we are to teach doctrine, not other materials. Paul warned of "itching ears" in the last days, when people will not endure sound doctrine, but will rather turn to fables (2 Timothy 4:3-4). We as gospel instructors, youth leaders and parents are to make sure our lessons are filled with doctrine, not cute stories or fun fables. This book will help you in this process.

Additionally, Nephi faithfully kept a record of the proceedings of his days—*all* of his days. We can, too. As we take the time to muse over important points and parts of the teaching process, we will be blessed with inspiration from on high. As we record that inspiration, like Nephi, we will strengthen not just those around us, but ourselves in the process. The end result is the following: "Nevertheless, ye are blessed, for the testimony which ye have borne is recorded in heaven for the angels to look upon; and they rejoice over you, and your sins are forgiven you" (D&C 62:3).

Throughout this book, I will often refer to the youth as students, and to instruction as taking place in the classroom. However, it is important to remember that parents are the most important teachers of all. The tips in this book can be easily used in the home during family scripture study, family home evenings, and even in those unplanned teaching moments. So let's get started!

No Throwaway Kids

Remember the worth of souls is great in the sight of God.
(D&C 18:10)

Most observers would have probably considered me a "throwaway kid"—a teen who failed in the spiritual matters of life. But not Brother Mask, my seminary teacher.

Brother Mask taught with fervor, treating all his students equally, regardless of their situation. Even me. My parents had left the Church and I had stopped attending most church meetings, other than release-time seminary. Brother Mask didn't seem to mind that I didn't dress right, nor that I didn't always know the answer to his questions. All students mattered to him. The day he passed out 3x5 index cards with his personal address on them meant more to me than he could have known.

The assignment was to mail him that card the day we either began serving a mission or the day we went through the temple to get married. Unfortunately, I had no belief that I could do either. I struggled with low self-worth and always figured those two goals were too high for me. To be honest, I thought I was expendable. But that day, as he handed me my card, I realized I might be wrong. If my seminary teacher, a man closer to God than anyone I knew, thought I could strive for those things, maybe, just maybe, I could. Happily I can report that his faith in me eventually bore fruit. Not only did I go on to serve a mission, I married in the temple.

My seminary teacher's early example of faith in me made an indelible mark on my heart. I now want to do the same for others. I choose to hold out hope and belief for every student who walks through the doorway of my classroom—regardless of how they respond to me or to the students around them. I will do all in my power to pray for all my students and to shower love upon them as we work together throughout the year.

I might never know which moment matters most to my students during our year together, but I know the Lord needs me to approach every day as a "3x5-index-card day" and to approach every student as worthy of receiving one.

The Battle is Real

You and I both know it: the battle fought in heaven continues here. It is raging, it is real. Satan is seeking to destroy the Lord's children, especially the most valiant. These valiant are present among us. Do we *really* know who stands before us in these 14- to 18-year-old bodies? Thus, is any student really too far out for us to reach or so difficult that we must actually give up? Disregarding the hair, disregarding the clothing, disregarding the attitude, deep down inside each student abides a child of God who just may be the next Saul-turned-Paul for the Lord.

> As for Saul, he made havock of the church, entering into every house, and haling men and women committed them to prison...
>
> Breathing out threatenings and slaughter against the disciples of the Lord, [Saul] went unto the high priest,

And desired of him letters to Damascus to the synagogues, that if he found any of this way, whether they were men or women, he might bring them bound unto Jerusalem.

And as he journeyed, he came near Damascus: and suddenly there shined round about him a light from heaven:

And he fell to the earth, and heard a voice saying unto him, Saul, Saul, why persecutest thou me?

And he said, Who art thou, Lord? And the Lord said, I am Jesus whom thou persecutest: it is hard for thee to kick against the pricks.

And he trembling and astonished said, Lord what wilt thou have me to do? And the Lord said unto him, Arise, and go into the city, and it shall be told thee what thou must do…

And there was a certain disciple at Damascus, named Ananias; and to him said the Lord in a vision, Ananias…

Go into the street which is called Straight, and enquire in the house of Judas for one called Saul…

Then Ananias answered, Lord, I have heard by many of this man, how much evil he hath done to thy saints at Jerusalem…

But the Lord said unto him, Go thy way: for he is a chosen vessel unto me, to bear my name before the Gentiles, and kings, and the children of Israel" (Acts 8:3; 9:1-6, 13, 15).

As teachers and leaders of youth, we mentor a chosen generation. Yet who we have before us might surprise us in their current condition.

How many of them might appear as modern-day Sauls, needing "light from heaven" to bring them around to their true purpose? We must teach with all the light we can muster; we must extend that light and love even to the kids some Church members might privately consider "throwaways."

And if we falter in the process? If our love or light runs out, we still have an ample supply to turn to, found within the veritable storehouse of the Lord's own heart. When our supply runs low, we can petition for compassion, for faith, for love. It is essential that we teach as the sons of Mosiah did, reaching outward to all.

The sons of Mosiah had been radical, even dangerous youth. Yet they morphed into missionaries who "were desirous that salvation should be declared to every creature, for they could not bear that any human soul should perish; yea, even the very thoughts that any soul should endure endless torment did cause them to quake and tremble" (Mosiah 28:3).

Powerful Teachers and Leaders of Youth

Perhaps it is easy for some to judge teens, simply because they dress as if they are "lost" or act as if they couldn't care less about spiritual matters. But the powerhouse teacher and youth leader wages an integral battle for the souls of these youth, gently nourishing all within their reach with the living waters of the gospel, overlooking none.

Others indeed may cast aside a "throwaway teen," yet the inspired teacher will not. Others at church may smile in a forced manner as the teen walks by, but powerful youth leaders do not. They reach out to these kids, taking their hands in gentle fellowship, even when class is done.

We can bring a positive elevation of hope into the lives of our youth—*all* of our youth—and we do it, not just in the classroom, but within the hallways of our students' hearts. This indeed is the goal of the powerful teacher, the goal of every youth leader: *not one youth left behind!* Not on our watch. We have entered into a partnership with the Lord Himself as we care for, *not* "throwaway kids," but for every potential "Paul."

Of all the things I saw and heard Brother Mask mentor and do during his years as my seminary teacher, the following powerful elements had the greatest impact on my life:

1. *He Put Christ First.* If there was one thing I knew about my seminary teacher, it was that Christ mattered to him. I knew this from the way he spoke about Him, to the stories of personal sacrifice to follow Him. More importantly, this gentle seminary teacher walked into the room and you knew he loved the Savior by how he treated you.

Arriving at this depth of spirit can be a challenge; we are human after all. Yet the sons of Mosiah carved out a clear pattern:

> Now these sons of Mosiah were with Alma at the time the angel first appeared unto him; therefore Alma did rejoice exceedingly to see his brethren; and what added more to his joy, they were still his brethren in the Lord; yea, and they had waxed strong in the knowledge of the truth; for they were men of a sound understanding and they had searched the scriptures diligently, that they might know the word of God. (Alma 17:2)

Not only had Brother Mask strongly "waxed" in the knowledge of the truth, he was a man of "sound understanding." He knew how to reach us—even me—with the gospel truths he taught and the personal experiences he shared. I will be forever grateful. This indeed was a man who put Christ first, especially in his gospel study, which leads me to the next point.

2. *He Searched the Scriptures Diligently.* I knew Christ came first in my seminary teacher's life, because my teacher put time in with his personal scriptures. I knew he did this, because as he shared perti-

nent stories of his experiences, those experiences came from his private study. As he shared these spiritual moments, the Spirit soared in our classroom, testifying not only of the truths this gentle man shared, but also of this man's love for his scriptures.

A love such as this comes from sustained daily scripture study. How hollow our testimonies ring if not substantiated with actual time spent within the pages of our own standard works. By setting aside personal time each day for private scholarship, we truly demonstrate to the Savior that, indeed, we put Him first in our lives. The young men and women we serve will feel this and rely upon it. It cannot be counterfeited. By putting the Savior first, we will receive great inspiration for handling even the most challenging of students. These promptings may come in surprising ways; yet as we hearken to them, the outcome will be glorious.

3. *He Prayed Consistently.* We read in Alma 17:3 that the sons of Mosiah "had given themselves to much prayer." How much do we look forward to supping with the Lord in prayer? Is prayer an assignment or actually a time of refreshment? If it's not something we give much of ourselves to, how can we share a truthful testimony as to its power?

I remember my seminary teacher telling the class how he and his wife had just suffered a miscarriage. He cried as he told us of the pain; he cried as he told us of the comfort that came from the Savior. I knew he was sincere when he bore testimony of prayer, because the Spirit of God permeated the class during his telling of it.

I will never forget his witness that praying full-heartedly to our Maker can assuage our troubled souls. I'm not sure if any other person in my life at that time could have gotten this message through to me as well as my seminary teacher did. And he was able to do it because he lived the message.

We, who work with the Lord's youth, need to pray how best to do this. People will pay hundreds or thousands of dollars to attend conferences and seminars to increase their power to communicate and to teach. Yet the Master Teacher allows us to approach Him for "free." Have you ever thought that perhaps we might be missing out on one of the most powerful seminars available—morning, mid-day, and night for the rest of our earthly lives! Yes, to become powerful teachers of today's youth, we must pray.

Putting Christ First

Our youth need powerful mentors that love the Lord and truly put Him first. They need powerhouse teachers and leaders who extend "3x5" cards of inspiration to even the most unlikely of kids. And they need us to do this at all times. But how do we balance all we must do, how do we fit it in?

Picture a teacher dumping a bunch of rocks out on a table in front of a class. Next to the rocks, he pours out pebbles. Next to the pebbles, he places a container of sand. Then he brings out a large mason jar.

Slowly he pours the sand into the glass jar, filling it almost to the top. Then he asks a student to come put the rocks and pebbles in the jar. The student tries, but they just won't fit. The professor then promises the student that if he listens, he will be able to fit all of it in.

Step by step the student carefully follows the instruction. To begin, he removes all the sand. He *then* places the largest items, the rocks, inside the jar. He shakes the jar to nestle the rocks lower. He scoops up the pebbles and drops them into the jar, shaking the jar so the pebbles "snug" themselves within the nooks and crannies of the rocks. As the last step, he pours the sand into the jar. The student has listened well. Tapping the jar on the tabletop, the sand sinks into every available crevice, allowing the student to top off the jar with the entire amount of remaining sand.

The analogy is clear. When we place Christ, the Rock, as the *first* and most important part of our lives, we then are better able to manage the other pieces of our lives. Anything left over is simply debris. One would think that we as youth leaders and teachers would have this down, but we are human after all.

When we put Christ first in our personal lives, through diligent discipleship, scripture study and prayer, our students will see clarity within our own lives and many will desire that for themselves. Additionally, and perhaps more importantly, we'll see each "Saul" for who they really are—a potential "Paul" in the making.

I know what it is like to be a "throwaway kid." I was one. Due in large measure to one very humble man, I am where I am today because he lived the message that each child of God matters and has a purpose. No child, no student, regardless of appearance or action, is a "throwaway kid"—not in the least. That concept—no throwaway kids—forms the purpose for this book: to help you to extend your very own "3x5 cards" to every youth who walks through the door of your classroom or enters the realm of your stewardship.

Your Ideas

In the next chapter, we will discuss the importance of a teacher's journal, a method of goal setting and evaluation of the progress you are making as you work with the youth. Each chapter in this book will have a series of reflective questions for you to ponder and answer. I encourage you to take the time to keep a teacher's journal and to think deeply about the answers to these questions. The more prayerfully you ponder the questions and the more detailed your answers, the more valuable your journal will become to you, both in your current teaching position and in the future.

❑ Why did that simple 3x5 card from the seminary teacher make such a difference to the author when she was a youth?

❑ Faith that is actually manifested through action, rather than simply talked about, tends to have greater impact. Why is that?

❑ Why is the adversary so interested in destroying today's youth?

❑ Why can it be so hard at times for adults to see spiritual potential in some of our youth?

❑ In your opinion, what does the Lord need teachers and leaders to do for today's young people?

❑ Some youth seem to handle the hormones and confusion of adolescence more easily than others. Why is this? What or who has given them extra ballast to help them create this balance in their lives?

❑ It might surprise a "throwaway teen" that they have been type-cast as such. From their perspective, what might be their story?

❑ Is there a "Saul" in your current class? If not, are there any in your ward or family? Who is it?

❑ As you ponder this potential "Paul," what kind of 3x5 cards of expressed faith and hope do you intend to hold out to them?

❑ Do you really believe that the Lord has the power to heal troubled souls?

❑ What can you, as a parent, teacher, or leader of youth, do when your faith falters in the process of dealing with a "Saul"-type soul?

❑ Why does putting Christ first in your own life make you better able to love and serve those who are challenging?

❑ How does studying the scriptures impact your ability to see another individual clearly?

❑ How can prayer contribute to this process? What is your experience with the power of prayer? If you feel your experience with prayer is lacking, what will you do to bring the power of prayer more deeply into your life?

❑ While fashioning your time together with your youth, it is very important that that you allow space for their inability to be perfect. What can you do to remind yourself of patience when a young man or woman under your stewardship falters or falls spiritually?

❑ Who is one person that held out a symbolic 3x5 card for you in your life? What was their greatest impact for you? How can you carry on their legacy?

❑ In pondering these thoughts, what do you feel the Lord would have you do this week to create 3x5 cards for your class, both literally and figuratively? Be detailed and specific in your answer.

Refilling the Well

(Enjoyment)

Wherefore, we shall have a perfect knowledge of all our guilt, and our uncleanness, and our nakedness; and the righteous shall have a perfect knowledge of their enjoyment, and their righteousness, being clothed with purity, yea, even with the robe of righteousness.   (2 Nephi 9:14)

When the request came from my bishop to teach seminary, I was a bit shocked. Even though I had long desired to teach for the Lord in this manner, I don't think I had ever believed I would have the opportunity. Instead, I taught in many other auxiliaries in the Church as I sought my degree in human resource development. I found great joy in helping others achieve their purpose here on earth and in helping them prepare to return to God's presence. But for years I was passed by as a variety of friends became the "privileged ones," serving as seminary teachers. I wistfully watched from a distance, longing to do the same. Who wouldn't consider being a seminary teacher a thing of great enjoyment—being the Lord's mouthpiece for his youth five days a week?

When the request one day came for *me* to serve as a seminary teacher, I felt both shock and excitement. Joy filled me as I contemplated enthusing young people about the gospel and all that the Lord has waiting for them. My enjoyment could scarcely be contained as I soon received lesson materials and the many spiritual "goodies" that seminary teachers use to augment their studies and classroom moments. I felt I was an eager tool for the Lord—to teach my students gospel principles.

Yet I also felt trepidation as I pondered the Lord's perspective of this responsibility I now had placed before me. I immediately went to work, writing down thoughts, deepening scripture study, and making plans on how I would entice the students who soon would be mine to teach about the gospel. Life was about to get really, really good. Oh, my naiveté!

Each teacher hits a few speed bumps along the path; I was no exception. I sure hit mine. I had suspected that as an early morning seminary teacher there would be a few moments of fatigue and perhaps even discouragement in the coming months, but I figured these speed impediments could be easily surmounted—completely forgetting the large pothole of an impediment the Lord had previously placed in my life: my physical health. For years I had enjoyed easy health, but not so any more. I now was dealing with chronic fatigue, fibromyalgia, and Chrohn's Disease. Guess what. Life was about to get very, very hard—since lack of sleep triggers each of these conditions and is what most early morning seminary teachers deal with all through the school year.

As I'd been excitedly preparing for an enjoyable seminary school year, I also had not taken into account the challenge of teaching sleepy-eyed teenagers who were functioning on four to six hours of nightly sleep themselves, due to their work and homework schedules. My own experience as a youth in seminary had been with released time seminary classes. It seemed nothing had prepared me for what I was about to experience. That beautiful enjoyment of serving as a seminary teacher slipped all too quickly from my grasp. I soon discovered why early morning seminary graduates talk about graduating from four years of "e.m." seminary as being equal to conquering heroes! I now was understanding it all too well. Rising before even the roosters do, day after day, takes its toll on a person, and it does so quickly.

Four days into the experience was all it took. The truth of the situation stared me in the face. I knew I now was looking up a very tall mountain and I wasn't quite sure how to traverse it for an entire year, let alone receive "a perfect knowledge of enjoyment." I quickly became worried that my body would give out, thus preventing my ability to receive the blessings mentioned in 2 Nephi 9:14.

In addition to my own physical challenges, I also was learning just how difficult it can be to inspire drowsy teenagers with the energy and power of the gospel, and to do it during what feels like a long, dark night. As all of this coalesced in my mind, I sought for ways to cope with the blessing/challenge of being an early morning seminary teacher. In the process, I realized that this parallels in so many ways the general challenges we face in this life. I struggled to make sure I didn't give in to the weight of the burden I was carrying, for I wanted to bring the gospel to my students in a way that would meet their needs. As I made that effort, the Lord helped me to endure. And yes, there were even days when my enthusiasm revived!

In so many ways, as teachers, leaders and parents, we will encounter difficulties along the way with our youth. For example, my health challenges continue even today. The teens in my early morning seminary class still continue to "drip" with sleep. Yet I have learned a valuable lesson from these impediments to joy. At one point during Lehi's "Tree of Life" dream, he traveled on his own for what he described as hours. "And it came to pass that...I beheld myself that I was in a dark and dreary waste. And after I had traveled for the space of many hours in darkness, I began to pray unto the Lord that he would have mercy on me, according to the multitude of his tender mercies" (1 Nephi 8:7-8). It was only after Lehi opened himself up to the Lord and prayed for an escape from the darkness, that he then could travel to where he needed to be—a place of delicious fruits, learning, advancement, and yes, joy.

Do we remember to pray when we encounter dark and dreary places during our tenure as gospel teachers? If a "speed bump" or impediment of some sort has caused us to lose enjoyment in our efforts, or if our sense of purpose has died, that can be a dark and dreary place in which to be. How long do we choose to wander in such a place of discouragement? Sometimes we may quickly remember to ask for assistance from God when we experience difficulty. But sometimes we forget to petition for aid and, like Lehi, we remain longer in the darkness, forgetting or unaware that there might be a solution, an escape. Through prayer, we can ask for mercy and help so that for us, like Lehi, the darkness will dissipate and we will see the fruits waiting—fruits of great learning and joy.

Some might claim there is no requirement that we experience enjoyment in our callings, that "enjoyment" is ancillary to our real purpose. Yet it would seem to me that a God of goodness and joy would have us walk in His same paths of joy and goodness. After all, weren't Adam and Eve (among others) told that the essence of life is to feel joy (2 Nephi 2:25; D&C 128:23; Moses 5:10)? Should enjoyment cease, just because we've entered into an agreement of service, especially difficult service? Is it not true that when we render meaningful service that we can feel some of the deepest senses of satisfaction known to mankind? There may not always be other rewards in this life for an obedient soul, but the righteous will have a perfect knowledge or sense of enjoyment.

Enjoyment can be attained even while in this life, even while struggling past our pathway's briars of fatigue or despair, our engine sputtering and barely alive. But before we can reach that point of joyful success, what if our enjoyment "tank" runs dry and we have no fuel left to conquer the speed bumps that show up in our path? What about that promised enjoyment then? Some call this experience "burnout." What is a gospel teacher to do when experiencing the empty fuel tank of burnout? It does happen, after all.

The answer lies in prayer, scripture study, and in one surprising tool: a teacher's journal. In addition to the endless fuel of prayer, we can revive ourselves with memories of our first sparks of energy, usually felt when starting a calling, but only if we record those experiences in the moment. Thus we see the wisdom in Church leaders' recommendations for keeping a journal. It does us good to review that initial excitement, that enthusiasm, and yes, even the nervousness we felt at the beginning of our service.

Could this ability to renew by reviewing our original thoughts be one perk for keeping a journal? Could it be that second only to prayer comes record-keeping as a renewable resource of energy and faith? That when our well of enthusiasm or hope has run dry, we can refuel with yesterday's memories of joy and excitement? If so, this book you hold in your hands will help you to renew your faith and refuel your energy by guiding you through ideas and exercises to help you create a valuable and very personal teacher's journal.

A common theme among great men and women seems to be a penchant for daily review through journal keeping. When people are willing to sit down and record their spiritual moments, thoughts, and perspectives, not only do they bless their posterity, but they also experience a cathartic process by participating in journal keeping.

At any point of burnout, how helpful it can be to read back on our early goals and intentions for service to our students. That is why it becomes almost essential for us to record in a teacher's journal our classroom activities, our hopes, our inspirations, and our experiences with our students. Not only will this clarify our purposes in the classroom, but these very records can refill our wells of inspiration when they run dry. Our written words can bring back joy—creating a form of a journaling "frontlet."

Frontlets, or phylacteries as they were called, served as remembrance tools for ancient Israelites, to help each individual remember the Lord in their lives. Our teacher's journal can do the same. When we record our goals, our lesson plans, our inspirations, our efforts *and* successes in the classroom, we are later rewarded with renewable fuel for the journey. Our written words become virtual frontlets of enthusiasm and hope, if we use them as such.

It is interesting to serve in the official capacity of "teacher" in the Church. There are very few callings that require more dedication or effort, if done well. At the end of each year, we seem to have things we're grateful we did and things we wish we had done differently. How helpful to record these thoughts! How important! Even if we do not serve in the same capacity, the next time we are asked to teach we can pull out our teacher's journal and infuse our current efforts with inspiration and guidance from our previous words.

By taking just a few minutes each week to write in your teacher's journal, you will give yourself a highly personalized and powerful wellspring of inspiration. Then during the year, if you've come upon a bump in the road which seems to throw you, driving you to the ground, you can come back to read and re-read your words, finding inspiration therein. If you run dry of hope or ideas (as many if not all teachers experience at some point), your journaling "frontlet" will have the power to revive the wellspring of enthusiasm you once felt.

The Lord promises that the individuals who faithfully hang on to what they have committed to do are the same individuals who eventually *will* receive a perfect enjoyment, "clothed with purity, yea, even with the robe of righteousness." (2 Nephi 9:14) Could the Lord give a better gift to any teacher? If we serve wholeheartedly, we will eventually receive the perfect knowledge that our efforts have been received by the Lord, even in the face of fatigue or dreary waste places. The Lord will dissipate the darkness as we turn to Him during our empty-tank moments.

The beautiful thing about all this is that the Lord never asks that we travel faster than we are able (Mosiah 4:27), but He does expect us to be consistent and diligent. As a result of our diligence, the prophet

Jacob promises us that we will be given the comforting "robe of right-eousness" from the Spirit (2 Nephi 9:14). As we use the tools given us, the Lord will lead us along the pathway to where pure joy waits.

Your Ideas

Take out your teacher's journal and record the answers to the following questions. Remember, the more deeply you prayerfully ponder the questions and the more detailed your answers, the more valuable your journal will become.

❑ Ponder your previous teaching experiences. What is one moment you'll never forget that later made it all worthwhile?

❑ Currently, your class's course of study is:

❑ From your perspective, what are the strengths of the students in your class?

❑ What do you love most about this group?

❑ What have you gained or what will you gain from interacting with your students?

❑ What legacy do you hope most to leave with them?

❑ In five years, what do you want them to be most grateful for?

❑ The greatest talent you personally bring to your teaching is your ability to:

❑ During your time together as a class, what three things do you want your students to obtain?

❑ What are your biggest worries for your students?

❑ When you were first asked to serve in this capacity, what do you remember feeling?

❑ And now your feelings are:

❑ If you were to describe an ability as the strongest reason you were put in this position, it would be:

❑ For most of us, our talents and abilities grow as we serve. Which of your talents have grown the most and why?

❑ Which of your abilities have grown beyond what you'd expected?

❑ When you were first called to serve, what was your greatest fear/excitement?

❑ What do you feel enthused about now?

❑ What do you worry about?

❑ What behavior are you currently using as an antidote to that worry?

❑ In the future, if you had this to do over again, what would you do differently?

❑ The best way to sum up your deepest desire for this calling would be?

❑ In pondering these thoughts, what do you feel the Lord would have you incorporate into your life this week to bring about a "perfect knowledge of…enjoyment" as mentioned in 2 Nephi 9:14?

3

Spiritual Bumblebees
(Faith)

And now, I, Moroni, would speak somewhat concerning these things; I would show unto the world that faith is things which are hoped for and not seen; wherefore, dispute not because ye see not, for ye receive no witness until after the trial of your faith. (Ether 12:6)

According to aerodynamic studies, a bumblebee's weight is too heavy for its tiny wings. Great effort has been made by many scientists to prove the impossibility of flight for a bumblebee. What a miracle it is then to see one in actual flight!

The Lord does not give up on His bumblebees here on this earth; regardless of their anatomical structure, He gives them time and the ability to fly. In many ways, these earthly bumblebees remind me of certain kinds of spiritual bumblebees in our classrooms.

You know the kind—those students who refuse to acknowledge their spiritual "wings," those youth whose lives are too attitudinal, heavy or "wrong" for their potential spiritual flight as sons or daughters of God. Or maybe you have spiritual bumblebees who reject nearly everything you teach. How can you get them to see and enjoy the potential of celestial flight?

At times, our faith can be tried by the actions or words of the youth in our class. Will we ever get through to them, we wonder? We will sometimes have students who do not appear as if they are listening, or we might have an entire class that is particularly hard to deal with. What if everything we try seems to fail? It is at that point our faith perhaps is most tried. How hard it can be to continue on, still believing in the power of the gospel to change souls.

During these times I am particularly inspired by the following scripture, where Moroni talks about faith being "on trial":

> And now, I, Moroni, would speak somewhat concerning these things; I would show unto the world that faith is things which are hoped for and not seen; wherefore, dispute not because ye see not, for ye receive no witness until after *the trial of your faith* (Ether 12:6; emphasis added).

Have you ever sat in on a court case or watched one on television? The dialogue from the TV show is probably more spectacular than that of an actual court case at trial, but there are commonalities.

In real court cases there is a judge and a defendant. Oftentimes there is evidence, and sometimes there is a jury. The defendant has been placed on trial to assess his activities on some level, in some arena. Once the trial is finished, the judge and/or jury make a decision as to whether the defendant is innocent or guilty.

Have you ever thought of your faith being on trial in this manner, as Moroni describes it? If there were a trial tomorrow and your manifestation of belief in your students were in the defendant's chair, what evidence would be there to support a claim that your faith exists on behalf of your students?

"Faith is things which are hoped for and not seen" (Ether 12:6). Those squirrelly boys who sit in the back of the classroom and make your life miserable—can you see them with an eye of faith? Can you imagine that one day they will be respectful and actually contribute to life? *Can you spiritually envision it?* Unfortunately, we are often blinded by what our physical eyes see.

Just what does it mean to see with an eye of faith? An ancient story of a young man illustrates this well. The king of Syria sent a youth to meet with the prophet Elisha. The young man soon felt frightened when he saw a host of "horses and chariots" surrounding the city. In fear he cried out to the prophet, "Alas, my master! how shall we do?" The response came, "Fear not: for they that be with us are more than they that be with them" (2 Kings 6:15-16). The prophet prayed for the young man, that his eyes might be opened.

A miracle occurred because of that prayer. "And the Lord opened the eyes of the young man; and he saw: and behold, the mountain was full of horses and chariots of fire round about Elisha" (2 Kings 6:17).

We, too, can pray that our youths' eyes will be opened to the possibilities and beauties of the gospel and to those who stand ready to help them. The fact that they are sitting in our class is a marvelous thing. We know not who they were before they came to this earth. Do we really dare prejudge them now? Maybe they are still baby bumblebees, unsure of (or perhaps unwilling to admit they have) their spiritual wings, but that does not mean they cannot achieve future flight.

Moroni said our faith would be "on trial." During the trial, we must not place ourselves in the seat of "judge," for only one true Judge exists. Instead, let us remain in our defendant's chair, continually putting forth true faith as proof of our love for Him and for His "bumblebee" students.

How will those students learn the lessons of faith if they do not see it manifested in our eyes and in our actions toward them? True, they have parents and others who love them. But we who serve them in a gospel capacity must consistently model faith in them and their abilities, even when the students themselves seem beyond help.

The Lord promises assistance. With prayer, the Lord will give us "the spirit of wisdom and revelation in the knowledge of him: The eyes of [our] understanding being enlightened; that [we] may know what is the hope of his calling, and what the riches of the glory of his inheritance in the saints, and what is the exceeding greatness of his power to [us] who believe" (Ephesians 1:17–19).

This great gift of wisdom and enlightenment does not come without effort on our part. But we can do it! There are many "whose faith was so exceedingly strong, even before Christ came, who could not be kept from within the veil, but truly saw with their eyes the things which they had beheld with an eye of faith, and they were glad" (Ether 12:19).

Could this not also apply to us as teachers? As youth leaders? To see with an eye of faith what lies deep within the youth of today? Are they not the noble and great ones spoken of by so many General Authorities? Regarding those who sit in our classes and create trouble, are we so sure they cannot spiritually fly, like so many scientists remark about the bumblebee?

Let us have hope and faith that all of our students, even the tough-to-handle ones, will have spiritual strength and power to fly. When we live full-of-faith lives, we too will be glad, like those in Ether's time. Our faith will have been proven. Our students will be able to "fly" after all.

Your Ideas

❑ How is it that the Lord is able to be patient with us while we're learning to "fly" spiritually?

❑ What aids the Lord in being so faith-full with us, when at times we can make such grievous errors?

❑ In pondering your current students, who could be judged as most like a "spiritual bumblebee"?

❑ In what ways do you think he or she might have been prejudged prior to this time, even within the Church?

❑ How do you think the Lord feels about this child of His and any judgments that might have been made?

❑ What do you feel the Lord might see as this child's greatest gifts?

❑ What ways can you utilize these gifts to benefit your class?

❑ What new responsibilities or opportunities might you present to this student to show them their value and great potential?

❑ Have you taken the time to get to know this student on an individual basis? If not, what are your plans to do so (is he or she playing in a sports game soon, etc.)?

❑ Close your eyes for just a moment and picture this "bumblebee" youth ten years in the future. Imagine that your faith has been brought to fruition. This youth is now a powerhouse adult and servant for the Lord. Describe this future leader in great detail.

❑ Now ponder your service and time with this youth. What ways can you modify your current activities to help bring about the reality of this future possibility?

❑ Who else in ward leadership could privately work with you to help build this youth?

❑ If this youth were with you right now, what do you think his or her true nature would want you to know? Who is he or she, really, in God's eyes?

❑ What gives you the belief that he or she can conquer their challenges in "spiritual flight"?

❑ What three things can you specifically pray for, concerning this youth?

❑ In what additional ways can you model patience and faith for your class as a whole?

❑ What goal would the Lord have you implement this week to begin this important work of teaching your "bumblebee(s)" to fly?

❑ Describe the specifics for this goal (i.e. time, place).

❑ What scripture helps you the most when working with the Lord's "spiritual bumblebees" and why?

Choosing Joy Over Fun
(Obedience)

Be firm in keeping the commandments wherewith I have commanded you; and if you do this, behold I grant unto you eternal life. (D&C 5:22)

Why must we be "firm in keeping the commandments?" Is it simply to avoid pain? That can't be true, because many prophets were obedient, yet suffered torture and other forms of deprivation *because* of their unyielding obedience to God. Thus, thinking this through, obedience does not always bring absence of pain, nor absence of trial. In fact, sometimes obedience summons the trial. There is much for our students to understand about obedience as they grow in appreciation of it.

Is our obedience simply to win a "prize," some perceived perk for having proven faithful to the God of this universe? That, too, is an unworkable stance, because sometimes perks in this life do not show up for the faithful. Often it appears that good people pass on without experiencing "fun" or achieving the "good things" in life. Some people openly laugh at those who refrain from sin, wrongly equating "fun" with joy. "Come on," they call, "get a little 'fun' in life."

So here is the question: Why is it that those who best know the Lord do not worry when immediate "fun" seems missing from rewards for gospel citizenship? How is it that the Lord's faithful speak in grateful tones for His mercies, even in the face of intense sufferings? Our students need to know. The prophets have told us that the days ahead will be intense. Are our students ready to remain obedient through it all, ignoring the hecklers and the temptors of this world?

After all Nephi went through, years later in retrospect he bore witness of the gentle goodness of the Lord (1 Nephi 1:1). Yet his two books in the Book of Mormon report horrifying acts of family violence enacted upon him by his brothers. How was it that he remained true and faithful to the Lord, in spite of great suffering? The anti-Nephi-Lehies had a similar perspective and level of obedience; yet a large number of them were slaughtered because of it (see Alma 24:15, 20–24).

Why is it that we sometimes wilt or faint when the spiritual heat of the day becomes intense? What can we do to strengthen ourselves so that we can be faithful to the Lord in all settings, just like Nephi, the anti-Nephi-Lehies, and so many other obedient souls in the scriptures? To imply that obedience always yields blessings in this life can be a disservice to our students. They need to understand that *after* the testing the blessings come.

Our students need to hear and know about God's amazing goodness and His presence. They need to understand why those who know Him best are obedient through any difficulty life may throw at them. Nephi placed desire for obedience to God above the desire for physical comfort. If our students can't yet comprehend this level of discipleship, what can we do to deepen their appreciation and understanding of it? Who wants to be fair-weather friends of the Lord, blown over by the slightest wind of indifference or physical trial? Not me, and I doubt not any of my students.

Nephi, the valiant anti-Nephi-Lehies, and other trustworthy saints throughout history have been willing to stand firm in spite of discomfort. What insights do they hold for us? For our students? What truths were they so sure of, that nothing moved them from their path towards the Most High? Our students desperately need this knowledge, because it will impact them for the rest of their earthly lives and eternal existence. Once they grasp for themselves the magnificence of Christ and what He did for them, the urgency of being faithful will fill their souls. This knowledge will lead to a love for their Redeemer that becomes more powerful than anything the adversary could throw their way. Our students need to know this and we are the ones called to teach them of it. When we live in a way that demonstrates the joy that comes from obedience, our students will see how to do it and be more likely to follow the path that leads to eternal life with God.

The days ahead will not be easy ones. Read any of the prophetic words from the Lord's selected spokesmen, both modern and ancient. Deeper troubles than we've yet known will soon be upon us, if not already beginning. Our students must know of God, of His goodness, and of the purpose of testing in this life. They need to understand and love the principle of obedience and what it will yield unto them. They need this knowledge deeply imbedded within them (as do we), so that when the final moments are upon them before Christ's coming, they will not fold under the weight of them.

Joseph Smith saw varying levels of faithfulness among those who were closest to him. Many individuals, both friends and associates, turned on him. Even though they had stood with him during historic times, the weight of discipleship felt too great. How is it they lost the joy that comes from a visionary mind and a willing, obedient heart?

More importantly, why did Joseph Smith not fail the Lord? How did he come to choose obedience, while being falsely accused, betrayed and imprisoned, seeing his children become ill and die because of the acts of others? He suffered through tarring and eventual martyrdom. What is it that Joseph Smith and other valiant souls knew (and know) that brings them to the altar of complete obedience? What understanding of God do they have that allows them to trust Him completely, a being that so many in the world accuse of absence from the very earth He created?

Our students deserve and need to know the answers to these questions. They don't just need to know these answers with their minds; they need to absorb them with their hearts. Picture each of these scenes: How *was* Nephi able to follow through to do what he had to do to obtain the brass plates? Why *were* the anti-Nephi-Lehies willing to die at the hands of their acquaintances? Why was Alma willing to give up the power of his judgeship and become solely a missionary? Why was John the Baptist willing to live an austere existence and to die for his witness of the living Christ? And why was Stephen, a man of faith, great wonders, power and miracles (Acts 6:8), willing to submit to being stoned? These are faithful souls, steady in their witness and love of God during times when that same God might appear absent. It is our job to first know this for ourselves and then to share it with our students. Finally, our students need to see our modern-day example of such willing obedience.

There was a reason we shouted for joy in the pre-earth life upon reviewing the possibilities here (Job 38:7). We knew the realities; I'm sure of it. God is a God of truth. He would not have lied as to the difficulties we would experience here. I'm positive we had understanding, at least in part, of what lay before us if we chose the plan of happiness presented to us. For example, my husband's patriarchal blessing mentions he had the opportunity to view the possibilities present on the earth, both good and ill, and he still chose to come and to fulfill a work while here. Again, our God is a God of truth. Can you imagine Him withholding essential knowledge before we made our choice? I think not. Knowing the possibilities, we *still* shouted for joy. It would seem apparent we had a wider perspective than what we now have.

The battle here rages. But amidst the suffering and anguish experienced in mortality, there really is joy that can await the faithful, even in this life. There are flowers to enliven the senses, foods to taste, birds to

hear, so much beauty to enjoy. And the relationships! Oh, the relationships of lasting love that we can build while here. Lucifer would have us
lose all of this, both now and in the eternities, by focusing on the sacrifices required of the faithful. He would also have us get so entangled in
his snares of sin that we forget there really is a way back. Thus, as
teachers we show up every day for class with our students—to teach
them of the plan of salvation, to teach them of the Redemption, and
especially to teach them of the significance of obedience.

When our students (and ourselves, for that matter) really understand the beauty of the Lord, His grace, His compassion, His wisdom,
His mercy—the descriptions could continue on—these same students
will far better grasp why the Lord's prophets have revered and adored
Him throughout the ages. Our students will want to please Him by
repenting of their sins and living a life of full-hearted obedience. The
individuals who have an undying love and awe for the Lord are those
who have taken the time to get to know Him in the scriptures, through
pondering and with prayer. As a result, these individuals become sons
and daughters in Christ.

> And now, it came to pass that when king Benjamin had
> made an end of speaking the words which had been
> delivered unto him by the angel of the Lord, that he cast
> his eyes round about on the multitude, and behold they
> had fallen to the earth, for the fear of the Lord had come
> upon them.
>
> And they had viewed themselves in their own carnal
> state, even less than the dust of the earth. And they all
> cried aloud with one voice, saying: O have mercy, and
> apply the atoning blood of Christ that we may receive
> forgiveness of our sins, and our hearts may be purified;
> for we believe in Jesus Christ, the Son of God, who

created heaven and earth, and all things; who shall come down among the children of men.

And it came to pass that after they had spoken these words the Spirit of the Lord came upon them, and they were filled with joy, having received a remission of their sins, and having peace of conscience, because of the exceeding faith which they had in Jesus Christ who should come, according to the words which king Benjamin had spoken unto them (Mosiah 4:1-3).

It is essential for our students to gain this experience! They do this by being firm in keeping the commandments, by choosing joy over fun.

Your Ideas

❑ What is your biggest worry for your students this week?

❑ As you contemplate the prophecies in the scriptures and given during various General Conferences, what do your students need most to prepare them for the times ahead?

❑ What might your students understand obedience to be?

❑ What is your role to help them prepare for full-hearted obedience to God?

❑ As you ponder these things, what impressions come to you as to where your students struggle the most with obedience?

❑ According to the Legacy Network, a national organization that fights to preserve the family, the largest group of consumers today viewing pornography is 12- to 17-year olds! How has the adversary accomplished this in such a relatively short period of time?

[Author's note: There may be youth that you know who silently suffer from this deadly affliction. There are Church resources to help such individuals. Visit www.providentliving.com and click on the "Social and Emotional Strength" link. Within that link you will have two options. Click either on "Ten Common Challenges Facing Families" and search

for "Pornography" in the list of ten challenges, or click on "Addiction Recovery." If an individual is struggling with pornography, it is not simply an issue of obedience, it is an issue of addiction—a specific and much more serious matter. Do not downplay or be casual with this difficulty.]

❑ President Hinckley has said, "The tide of evil flows. Today it has become a veritable flood. Most of us, living somewhat sheltered lives, have little idea of the vast dimensions of it" ("In Opposition to Evil," *Ensign*, Sept. 2004, p. 3). How can you arm your students with obedience to strengthen them against this "mounting tide of filth?"

❑ What is a scripture that comes to mind that could help an individual remember God during each choice made in this lifetime?

❑ How might it help your students to know that you are there for them, leading them in the sure and steady paths of obedience through life?

❑ In thinking of the difference you can make for your youth, what is one goal you feel inspired to implement this week to strengthen your students in obedience? What will you do to demonstrate a willing and obedient heart? How will you show them the loving nature of God?

❑ What are the specifics for this goal (time, place, etc.)?

One Is Too Many

(Spiritual Casualties)

We saw a vision of the sufferings of those with whom he made war and overcame. (D&C 76:30)

Elder Henry B. Eyring has stated: "Too many of our students become spiritual casualties….One such tragedy is one too many. And yet the troubles and the temptations our students faced just five years ago pale in comparison with what we see now, and even more difficult times are ahead….We need greater power to get the gospel down into the hearts and lives of our students" ("The Spirit Must Be Our Constant Companion" [in *An Evening with President Gordon B. Hinckley*, 7 Feb 2003], 1).

"One such tragedy is one too many." As parents, teachers and leaders, those clarion words ring in our ears. They haunt us. We cannot stand the thought that a student under our watch gets lost. This fuels the choices we make in preparation for being in front of our youth; it fuels the activities we engage in when we are not with them.

The prophets have foretold our day for eons. These same prophets who reveled in the glory and majesty of the kingdom set up in our day, also bemoaned the filthy reality that would saturate the world. We live during prophetic times and we are losing our youth to the conditions prophesied.

Thus, as teachers we arm ourselves in the full armor of God so that we "may be able to withstand in the evil day" (Ephesians 6:13). In fact, we stand ready at the front lines of the Lord's army by virtue of our callings as gospel teachers. We, as the Lord's teachers of truth, seek the constant companionship of the Spirit. We do not let a single day of teaching pass by without bearing witness to our students as to the need for our Redeemer and the need for living pure lives.

We understand how crucial it is that these youth choose to clothe themselves with spiritual armor in recognition of the adversary's fury. How important it is that they recognize that the adversary is playing for keeps. The adversary is roaming as an angry beast, eager for his prey. He celebrates when one falls, as do his angels. We read: "Wo, wo, wo unto this people; wo unto the inhabitants of the whole earth except they shall repent; for the devil laugheth and his angels rejoice…" (3 Nephi 9:2). And while Lucifer laughs, he lengthens his stride. He is ever seeking the destruction of all goodness and especially the destruction of God's priceless children.

As the Lord's teachers, we understand that Lucifer is deadly serious. He never sleeps. He is trying everything possible to pull down the elect of God. Lucifer is powerful and he is angry. Whereas some might minimize the overall part that Lucifer plays here on earth, Elder Eyring does not and neither do we. As gospel teachers, we are far too familiar with Lucifer's potent reality.

> And others will he pacify, and lull them away into carnal security, that they will say: All is well in Zion; yea, Zion prospereth, all is well—and thus the devil cheateth their souls, and leadeth them away carefully down to hell.
>
> And behold, others he flattereth away, and telleth them there is no hell; and he saith unto them: I am no devil,

for there is none—and thus he whispereth in their ears, until he grasps them with his awful chains, from whence there is no deliverance.

Yea, they are grasped with death, and hell;…

Therefore, wo be unto them that is at ease in Zion! Wo be unto him that crieth: All is well! (2 Nephi 28:21–25)

Life is not a game, where after the scoreboard lights go out and the crowd goes home, one drives to a convenience store to buy ice cream sandwiches. Not at all. This "game of life," as some call it, has been described in the scriptures as an actual war.

And while we were yet in the Spirit, the Lord commanded us that we should write the vision; for we beheld Satan, that old serpent, even the devil, who rebelled against God, and sought to take the kingdom of our God and his Christ—

Wherefore, he maketh war with the saints of God, and encompasseth them round about. (D&C 76:28–29)

We understand, and on some level our students need to understand, that Lucifer is working to destroy all that is valuable to the Father. Our students have one life to prove their faithfulness to the Lord. This is why choice matters. This is why we teach with such clarion voices. This is why we serve our youth the way we do. When they listen to us and refuse to be ensnared by the adversary, they will avoid unnecessary heartache, thus bringing greater peace to themselves, to their families, and to their Father in Heaven.

Elder Eyring has sounded the alert; Satan is winning over our youth. As Elder Eyring states, we must get the power and potency of the gospel into our students' hearts and lives so that they do not experience that which is described in D&C 76:30: "And we saw a vision of the *sufferings* of those with whom he made war and *overcame*." (emphasis added) Again, we have been told by Elder Eyring that we're losing some of our youth. Let us do all we can to put a stop to that today! Let us determine that this will never be said of our young men and women again. Let us lengthen our stride and make our plans to win this war. Obviously, our students will exercise their own agency; it always has been such and always will be. The gift of agency was one of several reasons over which the war in heaven was fought. The right to choose is given of God and we can only encourage and lead, but not force our students.

Perhaps there is more we can be doing as teachers to stop the hemorrhaging and loss of the Lord's most choice of souls. Here are a few suggestions to help ensure that you and your students are well-fortified with solid gospel armament:

1. Begin now to write your goals for the year. Select two or three things you want all your students to have gained by year-end. Write them on a note card and tape it to your bathroom mirror. Review those goals daily while getting dressed. Make mention of those goals during your personal prayers.

2. Analyze your goals and pray for the Lord to inspire you to implement them in practical, *measurable* ways in the classroom. For example, one overall goal might be: *Each of my students will have read the entire Doctrine & Covenants by the end of this year.* Now dissect that goal and, utilizing guidance from the Lord, break it up into twelve approaches—one per each month of the school year. Write these in your lesson planner—a monthly sub-goal associated with each overall goal. Your purpose in the classroom will be to determine how you can make these monthly goals measurable, attainable, and desirable for your students.

3. Take time to pray and ask for guidance to carry out your plan. How will you inspire and enthuse your students to actually *want* the fruits that attend each of these efforts? Your purpose as their teacher is to aid your students in these things, thereby helping them not to become casualties in this war being mounted by Satan.

A student who is not armed with daily scripture study, prayer, and service is a student who stands at risk in today's world. We want our students to take part in these activities. You may also feel prompted to incorporate other goals in your service with your students, utilizing the inspiration that will come from the Lord. Once you have seen what your students can do, your job as a teacher is to figure out how to enthuse them and support them in following through. The battle is real. The sides are drawn. Our students stand in the middle. Let's make sure the Lord's army wins—and that none of His soldiers is ever lost again.

Your Ideas

❑ In pondering this chapter, what are some ideas or thoughts that have come to your mind? What can you do to faithfully prepare your students against Lucifer's wiles?

❑ What are the characteristics of a teacher who is on guard against the tactics of the adversary? This would be a teacher who lives after the manner of Captain Moroni (see Alma 48), who is constantly alert to the conditions in the world and is actively strengthening self and students.

❑ How do your students know that you are here to teach, protect, and serve them?

❑ What are some manifestations that you are diligently doing so?

❑ Now for the opposite, what are the symptoms of a too-casual teacher in this regard?

❑ Might any of these signs or symptoms currently exist in your teaching?

❑ If so, what changes can you make to be able to faithfully prepare your students against Lucifer's trickery? These might be changes either during lesson preparation or during class time itself.

❑ What will you implement this week?

❑ How will you specifically measure improvement?

❑ What scripture best defines these changes?

❑ Now that you've had a chance to contemplate the topics of the past few chapters, what are your overall goals this year for your class? Make a list and then select your top three priorities.

❑ To make these three goals measurable, break them down into monthly approaches and write each month's goal in your teacher's planner. (See sample in Appendix, page 140)

❑ After pondering these thoughts, what one thing do you feel the Lord would have you focus on this week?

❑ How can you make this goal measurable and achievable?

Possibilities in Embryo

(Consecration)

That thy glory may rest down upon thy people, and upon this thy house, which we now dedicate to thee, that it may be sanctified and consecrated to be holy, and that thy holy presence may be continually in this house. (D&C 109:12)

Consecration is a serious thing. To be consecrated means to be set apart for a specific purpose or to be declared as sacred. When we accept the position to serve in the official capacity of "teacher," we agree to consecrate our talents and our time for the edification of our students. This is a serious commitment and should be taken as such, if we want to face the Lord after this life without shame for class time misspent. Auxiliary teachers and youth leaders are called of God and set apart, receiving special blessings inherent in the calling. Parents, seminary teachers and others who work with the youth may not have an "official" calling, but regardless of this fact, we are still teachers who must walk "in one" with the Lord. Our hearts should be consecrated to His service. We are asked to consecrate our talents and efforts for the edification and instruction of the Lord's youth.

These youth form a generation who are living out the prophetic visions of yesteryear. There will be more burdens and responsibilities placed upon their shoulders than perhaps any other generation in the history of the world. Ours is a time when Satan rages in the hearts of men. This is the time when filth is being poured out daily upon the inhabitants of the earth. Satan and his angels laugh to see the destruction we read about in our daily newspapers.

We have been told by our church leaders that these young men and women in our classes are among the most elect of the Lord's children, spiritual warriors walking through the portals of our classrooms. Yet chances are good they can't see what their true nature is—yet. Through our consecrated efforts, and those of others, the truth of who they are and their great missions will begin to unfold in their hearts. As a result, their lives will change, creating miracles for the Lord and for us here on earth at this time.

Is this not a cause for celebration, these possibilities in embryo that present themselves before us as our students? No wonder we desire to remain consecrated in our efforts, so that the Lord's glory *can* "rest down upon [this] people, and upon this [his] house…that [his] holy presence may be continually in this house" (D&C 109:12). We want that glory for our students and for ourselves—and we show our intentions by the preparation choices we make for class with our students. We *become* this desire by being fully consecrated.

Although sometimes our students' attitudes (especially those of our younger students) may be immature, repugnant, or otherwise less than desirable, these students are the Lord's next generation and as such, must rise to their own callings. While at times they might challenge us or what we teach them, we must remember they are not finished yet. For example, a high school freshman has only been baptized for about six years!

We call on all students to enrich their daily lives with eternal perspectives, reaching for higher purposes than perhaps they've yet achieved. These youth are our hope and the Lord's promise for a bright future, one in which they may have the opportunity to lead in preparation for the coming of Christ. These youth presumably will have grown to maturity by then and will need every bit of inspiration and wisdom we can muster for them in our classrooms today. These fourteen- to eighteen-year-olds may be the ones to greet the coming Lord. The lessons we give today must be the kind that strengthen them for their tomorrows.

Thus, as their leaders we need to live consecrated lives. We live in such a fashion that the Lord's glory rests easily down upon us and our classrooms wherever we may teach. We choose to live so that we can truthfully say we are dedicated to the Lord. As we so live, His presence will abide with us. Our students will feel and know it, and the results will be a victory for the Lord and His army.

The resounding result for all of us in this dedication is that when we are stumped in a lesson (perhaps by a question a kid has popped off), or when we are running out of time and still haven't made our point, or if we have a youth who is particularly challenging, the Lord will be with us. We will become receptive to the paths He would have us trod so that we may know the successes He would have us achieve. These blessings are available and waiting for all those willing to consecrate themselves in this manner. This is the promise for all teachers and people who choose to build a "house" with Him.

By giving the Lord a consecrated heart, he will give to us open minds, ready for new approaches that will bless and uplift our students in amazing ways. They will thus be strengthened appropriately for the days ahead. The Church will benefit, our students will benefit, and the entire world will be blessed by their presence and gifts.

So, yes, are we consecrated and about the process of building a "house" unto the Lord? Absolutely. As a result, the Spirit will come with great force into our classrooms and all will be edified thereby. The experience will be undeniable. It will happen for us as we choose to live dedicated lives. We do not need to be unbalanced or perfectionistic in this dedication. Rather, we will simply choose to live in such a manner that the Lord's glory will reside with us. We and our students will be made whole. The Lord and our hearts will be one. Just imagine the possibilities! All because we set about to dedicate and consecrate our activities and our classrooms to the Lord.

Your Ideas

❑ How does it feel when the Spirit comes so potently to a classroom that all students stop and truly pay attention?

❑ What are factors that help bring this to pass?

❑ When was the last time this happened in your class? Describe the scenario, the topic being discussed, and what seemed to have brought the Spirit?

❑ How often do your students need to feel these moments?

❑ What impedes these moments?

❑ How does lesson preparation aid these special moments?

❑ Within your personal lesson preparation, how much time do you feel should be given not just to reading, but also pondering what has been read?

❑ After reading 1 Nephi 11:1; 2 Nephi 4:15; Helaman 10:2; Moroni 10:3; D&C 128: and D&C 138:1–2, what thoughts come to mind about the importance of pondering?

❑ In your opinion, how much time should be given to prayer while preparing a lesson? How important is it to pray for help to shape the material for your students' specific needs?

❑ If you were training a new teacher for your class, what would you tell them regarding the importance of pondering and prayer to bring the Spirit?

❑ What part of a consecrated life do pondering and prayer play?

❑ What ideas would you share with the new teacher for increasing student enthusiasm in living such a life?

❑ What sacrifices are required to live a consecrated life?

❑ Do you feel you are currently living to this level?

❑ If not, what areas would you like to change?

❑ What measure does the Lord use to gauge our level of consecration?

❑ In pondering this subject, what do you feel the Lord would have you do this next week?

❑ How can you make it measurable and achievable?

Dissension in the Classroom
(Take Heed, Part 1)

Take heed therefore unto yourselves, and to all the flock, over the which the Holy Ghost hath made you overseers, to feed the church of God, which he hath purchased with his own blood. (Acts 20:28)

How inspiring is this—to know that the Lord purchased us and His church with His own blood. Thus, this is His religion, not ours. This is His gospel to teach, not ours to bargain with or dilute. Our purpose as teachers is to lift high what the Redeemer has done for us, in addition to teaching clearly His principles and doctrines. The backbone of Acts 20:28 is essential to the life of a teacher—to give heed to ourselves and our purpose. We have a "flock" assigned to us and we are to feed them. We also must frequently analyze how well we are fulfilling this commitment and make any required adjustments. How could we do otherwise? Christ has purchased us "with his own blood." What an eternally significant price tag and we dare not desecrate it with sloppy observance.

To take heed in the manner we ought, we need to be focused on why we are in the classroom in the first place. When focused in this way, the spirit will be free to flow unrestrained; we will be able carry our purposes through to the end. Yet there are things in a classroom that can prevent this from being fulfilled. Dissension is one of the biggest problems to afflict a classroom. Anything that brings dissension will make Spirit-driven moments difficult. We must avoid any form of contention, whether it is caused by backbiting, harsh comments, or two students bickering between themselves. Argumentative or unkind attitudes from one student toward another will become an impediment to what we desire for those we serve.

We cannot simply ignore dissension in the classroom, labeling it "inconsequential" and then moving forward with our lesson. Too many students' hearts have been silently injured because of unkind words flung at them, for example, during a supposedly fun game in class. Is this really what the Lord would have of our classroom moments? Aren't we meant to be stewards for all of His students—not just the confident and pretty ones? I believe most teachers do an excellent job, but I have also seen leaders that seem to allow backbiting or searing sarcasm from certain students. I'm not sure why, whether it is because the student is popular, or the child of a local church leader, or perhaps the teacher was intimidated by the student. Whatever the case may be, it is an unfortunate thing and it takes down the class as a whole.

Have you not seen the response on a student's face when another youth at church flings rude or condescending statements in their direction, while the adult in the classroom or social setting says nothing? Where are the file leaders who point the way toward Christ-like behavior? Are we really this oblivious or uncaring to the feelings of another? Is this really the way the flock of Christ behaves? Are we taking heed appropriately when we allow anything remotely like this to go on in our classrooms? Why would we stand idly by, mute, allowing such behavior towards one another? Should such sarcasm be allowed to reign in a classroom of God? Where is our stewardship over each individual sheep?

Oh, toughen up, some say unfeelingly. But words spoken, even in jest, have power to harm both the recipient and the sender. "Not that which goeth into the mouth defileth a man; but that which cometh out of the mouth, this defileth a man" (Matthew 15:11). True, our students are learning how to incorporate the gospel into their lives. True, our classrooms are laboratories, of sorts. But what kind of classroom would the Savior run? Do we really think He would sit back and let unkind comments be flung one toward another without modeling a better way?

Unkind and harsh ways are the ways of the world, but this is not the mode we seek as disciples of Jesus Christ. As teachers, we are called to be shepherds for all, not just for the strong. Some among us, including our students, have never had anyone stand for them. Christ has paid for each one with His blood and He needs such tender care from us for His flock. We've been given the responsibility to tend to them and to "feed" them. Thus, it is essential that we periodically assess the level of dissension in our classrooms.

The Lord, in His mercy, has provided a way for us to seek continual betterment. Through the merits of His grace and His support, we can be ever improving our stewardship. After a point, it can even become exhilarating to participate in a steady analysis of successful classroom techniques—for who doesn't want to improve for the Master!

Consider the following:

- What kind of a report card would the Lord give me this month?
- Am I truly holding up my shepherd's staff of example?
- What areas have I improved?
- What needs my attention?

When we err, it is usually unintentional. But even so, the issue needs to be corrected or adjusted. Airplane pilots understand the essential nature of micro-improvements. They call this "course correction." They are not bothered that it is a continual situation; in fact, if you asked them, they'd probably tell you they make corrections to their intended line of flight about 95% of the time.

Like those pilots, we teachers can welcome micro-improvements. Our students will see our example and lose the pain that some associate with being corrected. As gentle, but powerful teachers we really do welcome "course corrections." For example, I can teach each lesson with an open mind to the gentle influence of the Holy Spirit. By doing so, I am "taking heed"—evaluating both myself and the direction my class time is taking.

If I am on track, the Spirit will tell me. If I get off track, the Spirit will tell me. What a blessed event! Sometimes we've simply overlooked small things that need our attention. How grateful we can be for the power of the Holy Ghost, which quietly reminds us when we have been remiss. There stands no accusation, but instead a gentle prompting to change or modify our direction—a veritable "report card" from the Spirit of the Lord.

These kind, but truthful report cards from the Spirit are essential. How awful it would be to arrive at the judgment bar of God without ever having received one—for we all err and fall short. No, the Lord does not leave us to figure out life on our own, nor should we leave our students to do so. Instead, the Lord nudges us to make course corrections within our stewardship. If I am willing to check my flight trajectory each day while teaching, I can better ensure that we will arrive at the proper destination by the end of class. By taking heed, my students will have been watched over and correctly nurtured through gospel truths.

To watch for hurtful comments has been one of the most full-of-impact spiritual report cards the Spirit has given me during my years as a gospel teacher and leader. From this, I've learned better about the shepherd's art—the ability to gently guide the Lord's sheep from one side of a field to another. I've learned to steadily nudge my students in better directions—away from the cesspool of harsh comments and toward lush green fields of camaraderie and brotherhood. Will students always get along? Obviously not. But as I take heed for my little flock, the lands in which my students feed will be an oasis from the ugliness of a parched and raging world.

Christ has purchased us! One of the best ways we can show our gratitude is by gently caring for his flock and expecting appropriate behavior amongst our students toward one another. His words were simple and straight to the point: "By this shall all men know that ye are my disciples, if ye have love one to another" (John 13:35).

Your Ideas

❑ What does it mean to "take heed...unto yourselves"?

❑ What does it mean to "take heed...to all the flock"?

❑ What kind of activities does this imply on the part of the teacher?

❑ What is your purpose with the youth you serve?

❑ How does dissension derail this purpose or process?

❑ Why do some teachers ignore dissension?

❑ What is the long-term impact of ignoring contention or dissension among the youth?

❑ What forms of dissension are the most spiritually deadly?

❑ The finest of teachers continually watch for subtle signs from students, whether it is regarding levels of comprehension or signs of hurt. What are some ways you can apply this in your service with the youth?

❑ Why must you care for all in the flock, not just for those that are convenient or easy to love?

❑ What is the value of micro-corrections, whether for a plane's flight or for the spiritual direction in the lives of your youth?

❑ The more we heed the Spirit's guidance, the more it comes. Would you agree with this? Why or why not?

❑ How can you demonstrate your knowledge of the price Christ paid to redeem you?

❑ In which ways do you model this understanding for the youth in your life? In which ways do you intend to micro-correct and how?

❑ What are the dangers of micro-corrections and how could they backfire, thus injuring tender students? How can you handle micro-corrections more effectively?

❑ What do you feel the Lord would have you do this next week?

❑ How can you make it measurable and achievable?

Moderation and Balance
(Take Heed, Part 2)

*Take heed therefore unto yourselves, and to all the flock, over
the which the Holy Ghost hath made you overseers, to feed
the church of God, which he hath purchased with his own
blood.* (Acts 20:28)

I n the previous chapter, we discussed the importance taking heed of
any dissension which might exist in our classroom. But another
essential part of taking heed is that of watching for moderation and
balance. As teachers, we often want to give our all to lesson preparation
and to our students. But we are also spouses, mothers or fathers, and
friends. Some of us are working and/or going to school. Thus, last
month's "spiritual report card" might alert us to the fact that we have
become off-balance in a few of these categories. This, in and of itself,
might not disappoint the Lord, but ignoring the "report card" might.

For a teacher or leader who is devoted to their stewardship, it can
be challenging to balance classroom preparations with other commit-
ments. It can be hard to know when to stop. Personally, I would like
everything perfect for my lessons. Yet if I overlook the needs of my own
children during their formative years, who will pay later if they fail at the
things that matter most? The truthful answer to that question is: both
they and my broken heart.

I've seen teachers and leaders burn themselves out, in the name of their calling and to the exclusion of their own children. I've had problems with this myself. It can take a lifetime to learn when enough is enough. That is why prayer and living in sensitivity to the Spirit are so important. We must be ready and willing to give "heed" to the spiritual report cards the Spirit delivers.

An effective way to determine balance in our life can be quite simple. We sit down once a month to do some prayerful self-analysis. A good time for doing this might be while fasting each month. Take the time to write down your goals for the next four weeks. Look back on the goals you jotted down last month. Review the notes you previously wrote in your teacher's journal. Imagine that you are your spouse, your children, your friends, your employer or teacher. What grade would each of these individuals give you?

From this point, make some determinations. What are your greatest priorities for each of these stewardships in your life? You cannot be all things to all people, but you must be the right things to the right people. Most people spell the word love with the four letters "T-I-M-E." You will not be able to do everything and spiritually "go" everywhere you want in this year. But when you are like the pilot, willing to make "micro-corrections" throughout the month, you will arrive where you will find the greatest joy, comfort, and satisfaction.

By the way, have you determined yet just what your spiritual destination is for this year? What is it your family needs from you by the end of the year? What is it your class needs from you? Your work? Your school? Ponder these questions, study the scriptures, fast, and ask the Lord for His input. Once you know these points of destination, write them down in very specific terms in your teacher's journal. That which we think, we tend to become. That which we focus on, we tend to be drawn towards. When our purposes are actually recorded, we can consistently and easily do a flight check during our monthly planning pit stops. Again, that which we focus on, we usually achieve—or come very, very close.

Alma taught, "I know that he granteth unto men according to their desire…yea, I know that he allotteth unto men, yea, decreeth unto them decrees which are unalterable, according to their wills" (Alma 29:4).

The scriptures are replete with individuals who understood and lived this truth. They received their desires. For example, we read of Hannah's accomplished desire, "For this child I prayed; and the Lord hath given me my petition which I asked of him" (1 Samuel 1:27). Christ is quoted as saying, "Ask and it shall be given unto you; seek, and ye shall find; knock, and it shall be opened unto you" (Matthew 7:7). Luke records the same promise (Luke 11:9), as does Nephi during the time of Christ's coming to the Nephites (3 Nephi 14:7).

When we prayerfully set our specific purposes before us, they become undeniably clear. They remain with us and it is much more likely that we will achieve them. Thus we give our students and ourselves a gift by determining very specific goals—ones we can actually measure. For example, a seminary teacher could say, "By the end of the year, all of my youth will have memorized their scripture mastery verses." An institute teacher could say, "By the end of this semester, all of my students will have read the entire Old Testament." A young woman's leader might say, "All of my girls will receive their Young Womanhood medallion at the end of the next two years."

Measurable goals are more achievable, because we can continually monitor our actual progress and make the integral micro-corrections along the way. This is how we pay heed to the flock—by balancing, in moderation, goals which are achievable and easy to measure. By setting a purpose that is specific, rather than vague, we can measure our progress during our private monthly review sessions with the Spirit. Once we've set our specific purposes, we can then get started on *how* we will inspire the class enough that they will want to participate. We need never question if we are giving sufficient "heed" to our flock when we are following through with these consistent and balanced methods of assessment. We're proving that we are paying heed to our assignment in a way that is balanced and not over the top. Our focus will ensure that our efforts with our young men and women are timely, efficient, and effective.

In writing about balance and moderation, King Benjamin gives us one of the most comforting verses in all of scripture: "And see that all these things are done in wisdom and in order; for it is not requisite that a man should run faster than he has strength. And again, it is expedient that he should be diligent, that thereby he might win the prize; therefore, all things must be done in order" (Mosiah 4:27).

It is joyous to know that the Lord understands our hearts, our efforts, our abilities and energy levels, and the demands being placed upon us from other fronts. As we work toward applying ourselves for Him, we can rest assured that He understands just how far we really can go and just how much we really can do before we tire and can go no further. He will meet us wherever we tire and carry us the remaining distance. I know, for I have seen this happen in my own life.

One of the simplest ways to pay heed and to ensure balance in our efforts is to know what we are about. Questions to help define that balance might be along these lines: What does the Lord expect from my students? What does the Lord expect from me? What do I want my students to have gained from their time with me?

The answers to our questions become subtle "water marks" for our lives, quiet lines of demarcation against which we can measure our progress. Once we establish these water marks, we can step back a bit, knowing that if we are reaching those marks, we are doing a job sufficient to please the Lord. He does not ask for over-the-top shepherding exertion; He simply asks for spiritually-based, steady effort.

It is important to know that initially some of our flock may not want our guidance. That is okay. These students more than likely will come around once they truly know that we care—that we're not faking our concern. Their efforts at resisting us will soften as they begin to recognize the import of the standards we hold out. Our shepherd's staff of love and heed will begin to nurture them more than they might expect.

I want my students to know that I am serious in my duties. In fact, I tell them early on in the year that I stand before them as the Lord's witness and shepherd for His flock. As such, I can allow no backbiting of others, no rude comments, no rough-housing during any games we might play, etc. I also share why. I let them know that if there is anything that would impede the flow of the Spirit, I immediately address those things. I do all this on the same day that I share the purpose of our experience together—that purpose being to have them rise to their true potential. Just as a marathoner will train mile after mile to win the race, we as a class are in training to win a much more important race. I tell the youth that as all serious runners have a coach, I have been assigned to be their "coach," their protector, their shepherd.

They soon see that my purpose is to oversee our classroom experiences together, to ensure that they are richly taught in the Spirit of God. This will drive what we do in class. I share goals with them. I also stimulate brainstorming on developing their class goals. Why are they sitting here? Surprisingly, many of them have never processed this beyond "Because Dad and Mom told me to be here," or "Because this is where I'm supposed to be."

I want them to get past the surface nature of those answers. As such, I ask them what they see as roadblocks to classroom learning and how should we deal with them. I ask what will bring joyous moments and how can we work toward creating those moments as a class. I really expect the students to process this and become better for it—to own the fact that this is *their* class time and experience. What can they do to make sure they get the most out of it for their futures?

When they themselves have input in what it is that *they* want out of the experience, they are much more likely to be willing participants. To develop this, I have passed out brief surveys or interviews for them to fill out, to help them figure out why they are present in class. By finding out what they think, it also helps me gauge the maturity level of the class and helps me to know how quickly or slowly I might move regarding future spiritual topics. Then together, we blend their goals with mine to come up with our overall purpose.

Once we have arrived at an agreed upon (and well-announced) purpose, it becomes our class "mission statement" for the year (posted on a bulletin board). Each day, all of us can gauge ourselves and the lesson against our posted purpose or mission as a class. This comes in handy, should things get out of hand. I simply reference it, thus reminding the students that we do have a purpose and I aim to follow it. I do this whenever needed. I let them know that in so doing, I am paying "heed" to the flock of God and ensuring their spiritually safe arrival at the destination God has set out for us. They soon learn that this purpose exists and I follow it *because I love them and want them to succeed.*

When we as teachers establish our purposes early on, they become powerful as they effortlessly guide us toward our intended destinations. We then can teach to these stated "water marks," ensuring effective heed of ourselves and our flock. The Lord has given us the assignment to be the overseers of our students and to lead them to the spiritually rich fields of gospel truths. Therein, they will be able to feed safely and to be strengthened. Thus, we hold out the standards we have established as a class and let the students rise to them. The funny thing about most people is that this really works—people will rise to the level you expect from them.

That's why we teach our flock that we, as their shepherds, must take heed and feed them, and we do it all because we have been purchased with Christ's own blood. As they listen and obey, we all will be well fed and rejoice as one united flock!

Your Ideas

❑ What does the word "shepherd" bring to mind?

❑ Complete this thought: "Effective shepherds..." Write several sentences with this beginning. Cover how an effective shepherd might behave and think, what skills or strengths they may have, and the attitudes they exemplify.

❑ How does being an overseer of "the flock" compare to being a steward?

❑ List a minimum of five stewardships you currently have, in addition to that of being a teacher or youth leader.

❑ What does "balance" mean to you?

❑ People who live their life "in balance" do the following things:

❑ On a scale of 1 to 10 (10 being high), how do you feel you are currently balancing your stewardships?

❑ What are some of the ways you are balancing your endeavors well?

❑ Which area of stewardship feels most out of balance?

❑ In an ideal world, would you also be doing?

❑ In pondering these thoughts, what do you feel the Lord would have you add to your preparation or teaching?

❑ What do you feel He would have you do this week in particular?

❑ Whose face comes to mind as someone needing additional time and attention?

❑ What will you do this week to help meet their needs and to help balance the time spent in their behalf?

❑ The Lord loves you for your:

❑ What do you feel inspired to implement this week?

The Amazing Gift
(Prayer)

But behold, I say unto you that ye must pray always, and not faint; that ye must not perform any thing unto the Lord save in the first place ye shall pray unto the Father in the name of Christ, that he will consecrate thy performance unto thee, that thy performance may be for the welfare of thy soul.
(2 Nephi 32:9)

Powerful teachers pray. At least, we are supposed to be praying, both vocally and silently. Amulek taught:

Therefore may God grant unto you…that ye may begin to exercise your faith unto repentance, that ye begin to call upon his holy name, that he would have mercy upon you;

Yea, cry unto him for mercy; for he is mighty to save.

Yea, humble yourselves and continue in prayer unto him.

Cry unto him when ye are in your fields, yea, over all your flocks.

Cry unto him in your houses, yea, over all your household, both morning, mid-day, and evening.

Yea, cry unto him against the power of your enemies.

Yea, cry unto him against the devil, who is an enemy to all righteousness.

Cry unto him over the crops of your fields, that ye may prosper in them.

Cry over the flocks of your fields, that they may increase.

But this is not all; ye must pour out your souls in your closets, and your secret places, and in your wilderness.

Yea, and when you do not cry unto the Lord, let your hearts be full, drawn out in prayer unto him continually for your welfare, and also for the welfare of those who are around you. (Alma 34:17–27)

As teachers and leaders in the Church, we are to lead by example through our gospel-applied living. Otherwise we live as hypocrites, essentially saying, "Do as I say, not as I do."

What we do in private may not be shouted upon the rooftops until much later, but so much of what we do in our private hours lingers on our face while we are in public. Have you ever been in a room when a stranger walks in? You aren't quite sure what is so special about them or what they do with their waking hours, but upon their countenance and around their being exists a presence of goodness that is undeniable. You can see it in their eyes, you hear it in their voice, you feel it in the way they treat you. On some level, you just know they know Christ; for it is when we sup with the Lord individually that we carry away with us a portion of His grace. We can feel it, perhaps not be able to completely define it, but we can feel it.

This is how I want to be. This is how I want to live—and it starts by making time in my day for prayer. I love the song, "The Perfect Prayer," by Ty Lacy & Steve Siler. The lyrics of this song remind us that we don't need to worry if our prayer is not perfectly worded. All prayers are accepted of the Lord if they are sincere. The Lord wants to hear from us and we need to talk with Him; in so doing, His presence and strength are with us more fully. Without His strength, we may be deceived by the destroyer. Lucifer is powerful, but he is unable to do anything other than yield to those who know the Master. We get to know the Lord by communicating with Him in the private corridors of prayer.

There is much to pray about in this deep form of communion. We can thank the Lord for the privilege of witnessing of Him to our youth. We can thank the Lord for the freedom to teach. We can praise Him for giving us the strength and the bodies to do so. We can petition for assistance in our lesson preparations. We can pray for individual students in specific ways. We can pray that our class as a whole feels the Spirit, being moved by it as they walk into the classroom. We can ask that our young men and women develop a love and sense of camaraderie for each other. We can pray to better know the Lord's perspective on our students.

The difference between a gospel instructor who has found power through prayer and one who has not is remarkable. When we live the doctrine of sincere prayer, our youth will hear and feel of our experiences, they will see evidence of our testimonies and profound fervor that prayer really works. If we personally are not there yet in this knowledge, we keep praying until the moment arrives when we know with assurance that the Lord hears our prayers and responds appropriately. One of the best ways to track this is to record the desires we've prayed for, and then record the answers that come over time; doing so quickly opens one's eyes that indeed the Lord waits, hears, and answers His children's prayers.

How often do we think to pray for the students who are the troublemakers, those who resist us in class? Do we pray to have a softened heart towards the student who refuses to participate and for the student who delights in making others laugh (or rebel) rather than do the work assigned? How often do we include them with our personal needs while praying? If a student is irritating, selfish, or defiant, then prayer is the order of the day.

When I pray for the needy among my flock, the Lord will hear and will bless them beyond measure with what they (and I) truly need. We cannot always know what lurks within a truant child's heart, but we certainly can pray to the One who does. We can also petition that the Lord will bless us with wisdom beyond our years so that we can extend that wisdom through our interactions with those specific youth who challenge us most. We can seek to serve them more than most, for service will bring love into our hearts. With love, we can see more clearly and wisely. Thus, we can pray to be filled with compassion and charity—the love that never fails.

Prayer is an amazing gift that the Lord has given all of us—but could anyone need it more than a gospel teacher? Let us teach it not only to our young men and women, but avail ourselves of its privileges as well and to our advantage. It has been said that more is wrought in this world through prayer than we can ever know. Let's use this tool as an integral part of our teaching efforts. Then, as powerful shepherds, our service and performance will be consecrated to the welfare of our souls and the welfare of the youth we serve. Truly, prayer is an amazing gift.

Your Ideas

❑ What are your personal feelings about prayer?

❑ What are your personal experiences with prayer?

❑ When did you first learn about prayer? Were you a child? A convert? What were your initial thoughts?

❑ Why does the Lord give us the commandment to pray?

❑ Some people struggle with prayer. Do you? If so, why do you think this is sometimes difficult for you or for others?

❑ What stands between a grieving heart and potential solace? How can prayer help?

❑ Are there students in your class who might be silently grieving, unbeknownst to those around them?

❑ Why can prayer be so powerful?

❑ What are the impediments to powerful prayer?

❑ Why do you think the Lord allows us (and asks us) to pray in our own words?

❑ What might be the greatest surprise for some of your students to learn about prayer?

❑ What can you do to further open up the world of prayer for your students?

❑ When was the last time you prayed specifically for an individual student, as opposed to the class as a whole?

❑ Who was the student you prayed for? What did you petition?

❑ How long did you watch for the answer so you could later thank the Lord for receipt of it?

❑ How does recognizing and recording answers to your prayers increase your future ability to receive and to recognize the Lord's hand in your life?

❑ How does understanding this help your students' manner of prayer?

❑ In pondering about your students, which student comes to mind now as perhaps having the most struggles—whether in class or perhaps in a different setting?

❑ What can you specifically petition the Lord for, in behalf of this student?

❑ How often will you keep this request in mind? For how long?

❑ In pondering these thoughts, what do you feel the Lord would have you do this week?

❑ How can you make this effort measurable and achievable?

Climbing the Mountain of Truth
(Scriptures)

Verily, I say unto you, that woe shall come unto the inhabitants of the earth if they will not hearken unto my words; For hereafter you shall be ordained and go forth and deliver my words unto the children of men. Behold, if they will not believe my words, they would not believe you,…if it were possible that you should show them all these things which I have committed unto you. (D&C 5:5–7)

I t is comforting to know that God is in charge. After all, He who created the earth and who gave us hope by giving us His Only Begotten Son, knows what His purposes are. His promises are sure. Therefore, we set about as His teachers to proclaim those truths to all within our sphere of influence, including our students. We are to go forth and to deliver the words of the Lord with faithfulness and with exactness—regardless of whether the "hearer" receives us or not. We are to represent scriptural truth without the least bit of variance.

The scriptures contain the gospel. It would be important to ask therefore, "Do we use the scriptures as our text from which to teach?" Hopefully, the resounding answer is, "Absolutely!" To do anything else would be akin to carrying empty fire brigade buckets—the buckets would serve no purpose because they bring no water.

Any lesson we teach which does not specifically use the words from the scriptures themselves are empty lessons, similar to empty water buckets. We then become nothing more than motivational speakers, not gospel teachers. If I'm not using the actual scriptures in my lessons, my lessons will not contain the living water of Christ, ready to quench the internal fires of difficulty we all experience at different points in our lives.

True, a teacher's manual will contain creative ideas for applying the scriptures to our lives, but we need to make sure our lessons contain more than just those creative ideas. Our lessons must have time set aside for the students to read from and study the actual scriptures themselves. How else will they develop a taste and a thirst for the word of God, unless they experience it for themselves? It can be uplifting to hear someone talk about their adventures in the spirit-filled pages of the gospel, but it leaves a much deeper impression when we have those experiences for ourselves. Why not encourage and provide the opportunity for our students themselves to make the climb up the mount of truth to find the refreshing waters of Christ's gospel?

There are many ways to use the actual text of the scriptures to deliver the word of the Lord to our youth. We could provide time for a specific scriptural research topic for the entire class. We could give an individual scripture block to each student, who then shares their favorite verse from what they read. Students could spend quiet time writing in their journals their personal response to a given verse. The delivery method can change frequently, but the point is that each lesson provides students time within the scriptures.

There are other ways, also. Students might create a group "testament" journal, based upon each individual's testimony of a given scripture block about Christ. The students could make a group presentation to the class via a scriptural "reader's theater." Or they could simply share with their neighbor what they learned from what they read. All these methods point the students toward the text of the scriptures, the "real" manual for life. Each exposure helps the students process those scriptures on a deeper and more personal level.

It is essential that we assess how well we are using the scriptures in our lessons. How much time do we spend actually delivering the real words of the gospel, using the scriptures themselves as our text for class? Are we spending time talking *about* the scriptures or are we reading *from* them in class? Nothing contains the power and witness of the Lord as do the scriptures. Our students need to be in them.

An easy way to bring the word of God into the classroom is to pull out your scriptures, find a verse from the assigned reading block for the day, and begin reading those miraculous words of Christ. Or better yet, call on the students to take turns reading a few verses at a time. You don't even need to give an explanation. Simply begin reading from the targeted verses for the day. Soon enough, the sweet spirit of the Lord will permeate the classroom, providing a perfect lead-in to your lesson. A sweet tone of truth and knowledge has been brought into your classroom. What a way to begin!

As teachers within the body of Christ, we have been consecrated to teach the gospel to our students. Let us do so full-heartedly and well. Let us use the real text of life—the scriptures. They form a handbook of instruction so rare and valuable that men and women throughout the history of the world have been willing to die for what is contained on its pages. As the scriptures state in D&C 5:5-7, we do not have a say over whether or not our students believe the Lord's word. We simply have the responsibility to share it.

Your Ideas

❑ Why is reading from the scriptures so important?

❑ If a camera followed you last week in your classroom, how much time would it have recorded of your students actually using the scriptures in class, reading from them and discussing what they read?

❑ How much time would it have recorded you talking *about* the scriptures rather than reading *from* them?

❑ How often would that camera record the students being given a research topic whose answer(s) could only be found in the scriptures?

❑ What scripture application activities would the camera have recorded?

❑ How much time would the camera have recorded the students in private (silent) scripture study?

❑ In pondering uses of the scriptures in the classroom, what are some new and unique methods that come to mind?

❑ What happens within a student when allowed time to work directly from their own scriptures, rather than listening to the teacher talk about them?

❑ Does every student have their own scriptures with them during class time? If not, how soon will you remedy this?

❑ What does the ability to record new thoughts or understandings within their personal scriptures do for a student?

❑ What are your personal scripture study habits?

❑ What are your personal feelings about the value of scripture study?

❑ What is the most memorable experience you've had during personal scripture study?

❑ How can you share the enthusiasm of this particular experience with your class?

❑ In pondering these thoughts, what is one thing the Lord would like you to try this week in class?

❑ What are the specifics for this goal? How will you measure its success?

A Lasting Legacy of Truth
and Inspiration
(Record-keeping)

For we labor diligently to write, to persuade our children, and also our brethren, to believe in Christ, and to be reconciled to God. (2 Nephi 25:23)

We are to be record-keeping people. We discussed this briefly in a previous chapter. There are many, many reasons to keep a record or journal of our spiritual experiences. When we're in the midst of a challenge, it is all too easy for some of God's children to forget what the Lord has done for them during previous challenges. A record could help them remember His goodness toward them during those difficult times. Others doubt the Lord and His goodness and can't see His hand moving in their lives. A record could show the patterns of God's help for them. Still others forget how much their future posterity will need their thoughts, decisions, and results recorded so they too can avoid unnecessary heartache. A journal would remind them of this.

We, as powerful teachers, can make good use of record-keeping. When we begin to lose our grip on what matters most in our teaching, when we're scrambling to keep up or to maintain our spiritual footing, we can look back on the record we've made of our journey thus far and be glad. For therein we will find encouragement and sweetness to savor as we read of our triumphs over difficulties in the classroom. We might giggle at some of the fun we've had with our students. And we can sorrow and make room for improvement as we read of regrettable choices, whether made by ourselves or by those over whom we have stewardship.

Each of our students comes from a different gospel background. Some are new converts; others descend from a long line of faithful members. Regardless of their situation, all students need to understand the value of record-keeping and they need to hear it from us. Nephi stated the reason for his journal-keeping in 2 Nephi 25:23. He wanted his posterity to be shaped by his words and his absolute knowledge that Christ was real. In fact, he diligently kept not just one record, but two. Because of him and other faithful historian-prophets, we have the Book of Mormon to encourage and instruct us. Those who faithfully kept these records will receive much fruit for their labors.

In fact, Nephi's efforts become a guiding light on how to maintain a log of our lives. By recording the spiritual events we've had, the understandings, and even the doubts we've passed through, we can learn from our growth. Upon reviewing it, we can be strengthened privately. We will be better able to see the Lord's hand at work, as we read of our experiences and see the patterns fashioned throughout our lives.

Perhaps we do not struggle in seeing God's hand in our lives, but sometimes our students do. A journal can help remedy this. If we teach youth the importance of journals, by having one for each of them during class, they can record on a daily basis the spiritual experiences they are having. As they make a written record of the experience, later on in life they can reference that again and again, receiving strength from it.

On the first day of my class, each student receives their own spiral bound notebook. It has their name on the front and is full of empty pages. I explain that by the end of the year, they will have been able to fill these pages with their perspectives on anything and everything we've discussed and explored during the year. I give quiet time at the beginning of the class or during the middle or end (depending on the need) for them to record their private musings. I even go so far as to strap each journal with a thick rubber band—a symbolic version of "Fort Knox." This is to remind them that no one else will read their writings unless they give their permission.

It has been interesting to watch the students' faces throughout the year as they make these journals their own. Sometimes they want to share what they've written with others; at other times they do not. But during each of these journaling times, I explain that they are keeping a record from which their children and future grandchildren will read and quote. I ask that they be honest with themselves in the making of it.

As our students ponder and then record the times they've been moved by the Spirit, they clarify the events in their minds, thus making these experiences more accessible and understandable for future recall. This also builds a capacity to recognize and receive future inspiration on the part of the student. By recognizing these spiritual experiences and events, they are training themselves to be sensitive and to distinguish future ones.

What Nephi wrote we now call scripture. We revere and are grateful for his words. But from his perspective, he simply was obediently recording his witness of the spiritual experiences he'd had. We've been given the same counsel through the years from our leaders, to keep a record of our days, so that our posterity may read and be strengthened thereby. We don't need to present a dishonest portrayal of who we are; Nephi didn't. No, we are simply to record the spiritual moments as they come. Our students need to know they have this same responsibility—to record those things which matter most. We, as their teachers, can provide the means and the example by keeping our own journals.

Without these priceless records, the experiences hard-won through the rigors of life all too soon fade, no longer ready for recall. They become, at best, nothing more than a mild memory with lost potency. Spoken words soon dim; the written word remains. We gain a testimony of journal keeping by keeping a journal. And in truth, we inspire our students to do so by our personal example. When we are faithfully journaling, we can't help but share the wonder of the experience with our students. Before we know it, we will have mentored a new generation of record-keepers. They in turn will bless their descendants as did Nephi through their writings—all because they had a teacher who lived the inspired precept of record-keeping.

It shouldn't be too hard for us to set the example. As teachers, we really do need the quiet, the respite, the inner peace that daily reflection from journal keeping brings. Believe it or not, studies have shown that those who keep some form of a diary experience less stress and more peace on a consistent level than those who do not.

Our journal might be as simple as a spiral-bound notebook, full of jottings and musings, or it might be an elegant, leather-bound book with gilded pages. It doesn't really matter. What does matter is that we are keeping a record of our life, including our teaching sojourns alongside our other experiences we are garnering. Our posterity deserves to know of these moments, how we fought our battles, and how we sought to follow Christ. In doing so, we leave a lasting legacy of truth and inspiration.

Not all moments in our lives will be "pretty" ones; neither were Nephi's. Yet he shaped his descendants for all of eternity by recording in simple and honest fashion the proceedings of his day. Imagine the impact on our students' lives as we share in excited tones an event we've recently recorded in our personal journal. From the expressions on our face and the tone of our voice, they will sense the excitement and value of the experience.

Our students need to be keeping these records. Why? Because it will tune them to the finer frequencies of life, where the Spirit and the Lord travel. They will become more and more able to recognize the Lord's hand in their life as they seek to record the spiritual moments they've experienced. Does any better fruit exist than that?

Your Ideas

❑ If someone didn't know you personally, but only knew of you through your life's records up until now, what would be assumed about you?

❑ Are you satisfied thus far with the record you've left of your life?

❑ As you are faithful in recording your thoughts, hopes, desires, worries, spiritual insights, problem-solving methods, etc., your children and posterity will gain much. What do you see as the greatest gift this will bring?

❑ What is the overall impact of these records?

❑ What serves as your current journal?

❑ The last time you wrote in it was...

❑ How much of your spiritual experiences, dreams, ponderings, testimonies, etc., have you actually recorded for your posterity?

❑ There are a lot of ways to keep a record: a journal with words (such as the traditional diary), a record through photo collages and captions; a compilation of copied letters sent to others; writing songs, poetry, etc. Your preferred method of record-keeping is:

❑ In your opinion, which method is most effective in conveying your witness that Jesus is the Christ?

❑ Nephi kept two "journals"—his large plates (historical record) and his small plates (spiritual record). In pondering this, if you ever decided to keep two sets of personal records, what would be the focus of each one?

❑ As long as your posterity can understand what mattered most to you, how you solved your challenges, and where your heart was regarding the Lord, they will be well-served. If you contemplated keeping a different form of a record, what would it be?

❑ If you keep your journal on the computer or online, when was the last time you backed it up (to ensure it couldn't be "lost")?

❑ What benefit does it bring you to be up-to-date in your personal record of your life?

❑ The prophets have taught that keeping a record of your life is important. This is even more so with recording your gospel teaching moments, lessons, and spiritual thoughts. What can you do to ensure you follow this sage advice?

❑ Motivational experts recommend that to be successful in any endeavor, we should select a consistent time of day and place for accomplishment of the desired activity. When you consider setting aside a few minutes each day to write, what time works best for you (be specific)?

❑ For just a moment, close your eyes and picture the perfect writing place—a place that is easily accessed on a daily basis, where you would be free to pour out your heart. Where is this place?

❑ Does a place like this exist for you currently?

❑ If not, what is keeping you from creating it?

❑ What can or will you do to create a writing place for you to ensure that you record the important moments in your life for your posterity?

❑ Regardless of whether something is difficult or not, sometimes we just need to do it. What are the best ways to model and teach this to your students?

❑ In pondering these things, what would the Lord have you specifically do this week?

❑ How can you make this measurable, to ensure your success?

When You're Green, You Grow
(Humility)

As ye have come to the knowledge of the glory of God,…even so I would that ye should…always retain in remembrance, the greatness of God, and your own nothingness, and his goodness and long-suffering towards you,…humble yourselves even in the depths of humility, calling on the name of the Lord daily, and standing steadfastly in the faith of that which is to come, which was spoken by the mouth of the angel. (Mosiah 4:11)

As a new missionary, I was wide-eyed about everything. Even the food in the Missionary Training Center felt like Christmas, because I had finally done it! I had become a missionary for the Lord. For years I had wanted to serve Him full time and now I was here. The hard mattresses in the dorm rooms, the long days of language learning, the new rules and regulations, all of it had a mist of wonder to it which enveloped life in the MTC in wonderful-ness.

Hmm. As the work increased, the mist of wonder soon faded. My early journal entries began to contain comments like, "Seventeen more *months* of this? How am I ever going to make it?" But then the despair turned to a confidence that was hard to ignore. After I had been at the MTC for nearly two months, I had it all down. I no longer felt like a greenie—and boy, did it feel good!

I don't think I was the only missionary in my group who felt that way. We were all beginning to feel a little smug and overconfident. No wonder one of the MTC teachers shared what he did one Sunday evening. We were sitting in a training meeting in one of the many austere MTC classrooms and he suddenly said, "You sisters and elders may feel you know it all now. Just wait till you get out to the mission field. You'll be back to being 'green.' You may not like the feeling, but it's actually the best thing in the world. Remember this one thing: *When you're green, you grow. When you're ripe…you rot!*"

The expressions on our faces must have amused him, because he chuckled as he looked at us. He kindly went on to explain that being "green" is a good thing. When we're "green" at something, we tend to be more humble. We don't think we know it all. We are more likely to ask for guidance, thus improving our overall effect. We are more tolerable to be around. As a result, the Spirit is far more likely to be with us.

On the other hand, when we begin to think we've learned all there is to know, when we think we need no more instruction because of our "seniority," we stop growing and begin to "rot." The teacher went on to explain the importance of retaining in remembrance our need for the Lord at all times—even if we've become a "senior" companion, leading and making the final decisions for the companionship.

His insightful words have remained in my mind for years. "When you're green, you grow; when you're ripe, you rot!" seems to apply to much more than just missionaries. I liken this a bit to teachers who have been teaching in the classroom for many years. There oftentimes begins to sneak in (sometimes unbeknownst to us), a bit of an attitude that we no longer need to attend our teacher training meetings, coupled with thoughts like, "What on earth could another visit from a teaching supervisor show me that I don't already know?" Ouch!

When Christ mentioned at the Last Supper that one would betray Him, the humility of His disciples is amazing. They immediately 'self-checked.' "Lord, is it I?" all but one asked. What an astonishing portrayal of open-hearted servants! Yet this is the purer mentality that all powerful teachers strive for. We want to maintain this kind of humility. If a leader needs to instruct us as to our teaching techniques, so be it;

we rejoice in the new knowledge. Who cares if we have more years of teaching experience? We want to remain open to anything we can learn that would make our time with our students more effective.

How sad if we refuse to have this kind of yielding way about us. How frightening to shut ourselves off from possible inspiration from others, even if younger or less experienced. The Lord accomplished His works through a young man named Joseph Smith. He certainly has the power to work through others who are young or less tested and tried than we are. The Spirit will work through anyone, if they are living a pure life. We want to receive all that the Spirit will send in our direction! We, as powerful teachers, choose to stay green, not rot, and to be open to instruction. Thus we attend all in-services possible and seek enlightenment from those called to instruct us.

I think often how there is only one perfect Teacher. So by all means, I desire to stay "green" so that I can be taught by the Master Himself and by those who serve Him. I *want* the Spirit to tell me where and how I can improve as I stay open to all efforts to give me the instruction I need. The most horrible thing I can imagine is to arrive before the judgment seat of God and find out how much I missed simply because I stopped attending in-service meetings, thus becoming "rotten" in my pride.

If we can't run the risk of finding out what improvement still awaits in our teaching approaches (or in any other part of life, for that matter), where will we end up? Far better to learn new ways to reach our students—perhaps more effective ways that bear more fruit—than to insist on doing things our way or not at all. This then, to me, epitomizes humility. This is the ideal of dependency on the Lord in all matters. Thus we say with great relish every day of our lives, as the Lord's teachers and leaders of youth, "I am OH so green!"

Your Ideas

❑ What does staying "green" mean to you?

❑ Why do you think the MTC instructor felt the need to teach this principle?

❑ Why might it be difficult for some people to stay "green"?

❑ What is the benefit of "greenness" (or humility) when serving in a church capacity?

❑ One way to stay green is to stay open to feedback. In what ways has this been easy for you in the past?

❑ In what ways has it been difficult for you to accept feedback?

❑ If you were speaking with someone who struggled with accepting feedback, what would you share with them?

❑ Why do some people rejoice in feedback? Why do they easily embrace it?

❑ In pondering this, what are some ways you can share the beauty of humility with your class? How can you help them to understand all that humility opens up to them?

❑ Why is it hard to tune in to spiritual promptings if you're not humble?

❑ What is the value of feedback in the Lord's mind?

❑ Why would He want you to be open to suggestions for improvement?

❑ Why are some people threatened by feedback?

❑ How does the presence of love help in the reception or the delivery of true feedback (not just negative criticism)?

❑ How will your heart feel when it's in a "green" state?

❑ What are some ways you can implement staying "green" this week?

❑ What are some measurable ways to monitor success in "greenness"?

❑ In pondering these thoughts, what ideas come to mind, either for yourself or your class?

❑ What is one thing you would like to try this week?

❑ How will you measure its success?

A Flock of One-Hearted People
(Unity)

There shall be one fold, and one shepherd.
(John 10:16)

We are to be unified as a church body. This does not come as much of a surprise to many members. Even the youth have heard this taught. We read in D&C 38:27, "...Be one; and if ye are not one ye are not mine." This standard exists even more deeply for those who have made temple covenants. From the moment God gave the command, "Let the waters under heaven be gathered together unto *one* place, and let the dry land *appear*" (Genesis 1:9, emphasis added), His desire for unity has been apparent. There is a type in this thing. The Lord wants mankind to follow suit in positive ways. We too are to be gathered together unto *one* place spiritually, with good works *appearing* as a result.

There is potency in oneness. In the scriptures, we can see examples of oneness leading to both good and evil. For example, in Genesis 2:23-24, Adam states his new understanding that he and his wife were to become one flesh. This statement becomes for us a veritable symbol of singular purpose and creation in the sacred and holy state of marriage.

Yet oneness in purpose can lead to devastating choices. In Genesis 11 we read where the Lord's children became one in evil intent, working to create a tower to reach to heaven. The Lord felt that this necessitated action; He restrained their results in a rather large way (see Genesis 11:6-7 and Ether 1:33). Be it for good or evil, the inherent power of "oneness" is mighty.

The Lord knows this. That is why He gave the command to Abraham, Isaac, and all those of the Abrahamic covenant in ancient days that they were to remain separate from the Gentiles. They were only to join their children in marriage to those of the covenant.

What is it about oneness that the Lord has always known and that we need to know today? What makes unity so powerful? And what can it do for our students?

A professor from one of my Organizational Behavior classes at Brigham Young University was quite clear on this subject. She spoke a great deal about "group think" (rhetorical talk for being one in purpose). She referenced example after historical example of what people would do in a group that they would never do alone. Be it "mob mentality" which causes crowd hysteria, looting and pillaging after a natural disaster, or "positive peer influence" which encourages a youth to serve a mission, the act of being "one" with a group brings about powerful results. Our students need to understand this. We need to help them gain positive unity.

Many of our youth have never felt "at one" with anyone. Thus, if they have not felt this way with any individual whom they have *seen*, how can they understand how to become one with the Lord, someone they haven't seen? Yet the Lord asks for us to become one with Him. We read, "I am Jesus Christ, the Son of God, who was crucified for the sins of the world, even as many as will believe on my name, that they may become the sons of God, even one in me as I am one in the Father, as the Father is one in me, that we may be one" (D&C 35:2). This is a tall order for an adult, let alone a youth, and especially for a youth who is emotionally adrift.

The joy is tremendous for the soul eager and desirous for this union. We, as teachers, become the guides on the path toward this oneness. We can lead students to this discovery! We can open a world of wonder and help them understand the beauty and peace that comes to one who is at one with their God.

How do we do this? It starts by the comfort we provide them through our steadiness with them. Through our look of compassion, the smile on our face when they walk through the door, the steady handshake we extend them. All of these components will work toward helping our students gain positive friendships with those around them and will open up more of a feeling of being "at one."

Ideally these steady and inspiring relationships should begin with the nuclear unit of the family. We always look to the parents to lead out for their children. As youth teachers and leaders, we simply provide an auxiliary aid to help the youth desire to be part of the "fold of Christ." Just think of the possibilities. By nurturing our students and building an ideal "fold" within the walls of our classroom, we can aid in creating a change in their hearts for an eternity.

By watching to ensure that our manners toward each other are kind and positive ones, our "fold" will be a flock that the student looks to for strength to face his day. You hear this from many youth; we want to be able to hear it from all of them! We want *each* student to look forward to time with us, to look forward to class each day. When each young man or woman finally leaves our flock, they will have been strengthened by experiencing this "oneness." They will be ready to set the example of "oneness" and to care for others of God's children.

Not only will this atmosphere of unity in our classrooms help our youth learn of the joys that come when living after such a manner, hopefully they will have become enthused about offering this to others. The fruits of "oneness" are eternally joyful. Who would not want to invite others to taste of them, once this knowledge has become deeply woven into the heart?

My favorite scripture is found in 1 John 4:19. We read, "We love him, because he first loved us." Now *there* is a mission statement for a flock of "one-hearted" people! In moving toward this gently, day after day, we will know the wonders of living as one fold, having one shepherd, and living in love. The power and impact upon the world will be remarkable.

Your Ideas

❑ Ask your class for their ideas on how to become "one." List their suggestions in your teacher's journal.

❑ What are your students doing for each other that demonstrate being of "one heart"?

❑ What are some examples of support and respect that you extend toward your students?

❑ What kind of spirit do these activities bring to the classroom? to the lives of your students? to your life?

❑ How much "oneness" do you extend toward your own church leaders, even if disagreeing with a policy decision that has been made or some other choice you disagree with?

❑ Brainstorm ways to bring a feeling of unity to your students. What are some new approaches that come to mind?

❑ When you've asked your students to do something and they don't want to do it, what can you do to bring about the spirit of unity?

❑ How does love factor into the spirit of unity, both on the part of the student and on the part of the teacher?

❑ Why are we to support one another within the fold of Christ?

❑ How do you model a spirit of oneness and unity for your class? for your own family?

❑ What are some of your unique strengths and abilities that can help create unity in the classroom?

❑ What are some of your students' unique strengths and abilities that can help create unity in the classroom?

❑ In a church of varied personalities, these gifts are particularly important because:

❑ In contemplating the strengths the Lord has given you personally, and knowing that you might have felt frustrated at times with others in the Church, how can you help your students during times they do not feel "at one" with others?

❑ In pondering these things, what do you feel the Lord would have you do this week?

❑ How can you make this measurable and achievable, so that it comes to pass?

14

Lives of Righteous Choices
(Seek Early)

With my soul have I desired thee in the night; yea, with my spirit within me will I seek thee early: for when thy judgments are in the earth the inhabitants of the world will learn righteousness. (Isaiah 26:9)

One can only imagine the world Isaiah lived in. Historical records point to the political and spiritual difficulties his society had created. Isaiah himself, upon receiving his call as the Lord's spokesperson, felt impure. He said, "Woe is me! For I am undone; because I am a man of unclean lips, and I dwell in the midst of a people of unclean lips: for mine eyes have seen the King, the Lord of hosts" (Isaiah 6:5). The Israelites of that time were engaging in far more serious sins than that of being foul-mouthed, but this is an excellent illustration of Isaiah's chagrin upon receiving his call.

The Lord resolved Isaiah's impurity. We read that in his visionary call, a seraphim came to him with a live coal, a symbol of cleansing, and laid it upon Isaiah's mouth. Isaiah reports that his iniquity was removed, his sin purged (Isaiah 6:6-7). When the call came for service, Isaiah immediately volunteered. His assignment? A difficult one indeed. He was called to preach to a people the Lord knew would refuse to listen. Yet Isaiah was to continue in this assignment until the cities were destroyed, until the land was desolate (Isaiah 6:8-11). Not a particularly glamorous mission, yet we do not read of any complaint from Isaiah.

Isaiah's record is among the most quoted of any prophet. Is it any wonder, since his entire message seems to be one of purity, righteousness, and complete surrender to God? Isn't this our message, as the Lord's ambassadors to His youth? Seek the Lord early!

We want our young men and women to understand that when we seek pure lives of righteous choices, and surrender to the glorious will and perspective of the Father, our circumstances will improve in amazing ways. Prosperity enters in, in many forms. Indeed, abundance of goodness and other blessings will know no end. The Author of the universe is at the center of all good and has promised to send blessings to those who are faithful and true to Him. Our students need to hear that as we obey the God of eternity, He will gladly open the floodgates to rewards we can only begin to imagine, whether in this life or the next.

Thus, as gospel instructors, we ourselves must live according to the counsel of Isaiah (Isaiah 26:9), desiring the Lord earlier, rather than later. His judgments are coming, they have already begun. His proclaimed vengeance against those who despise Him will be felt, and according to prophetic statements (both ancient and modern), it will not be pretty. As in Isaiah's time, cities will be left vacant, the land will be left desolate in many locations.

We find safety when we seek the Lord early. The Lord's judgments in the earth will not come upon us when with our souls we have desired the Lord "in the night" and "early" (ibid.) As we teach our youth these things, we aid the Lord in alerting His children. As our youth receive His words *and* hearken, His judgments will be removed from them. Isaiah stated it so succinctly: the "inhabitants of the world will learn righteousness" (ibid.) May our youth be part of that vision!

Your Ideas

❑ What do you desire for your students?

❑ What is the most important part of a student's experience in your class?

❑ When your youth walk away from the last day of class with you, what will you have ensured they know? What will they take with them to see them through the rest of their lives?

❑ What must happen within a youth's heart for them to be eager to set aside the natural man and to hearken to the counsels of God?

❑ What can you do to enable a student to seek the Lord early?

❑ What kind of support does a young man or woman need when they make the decision to put the Lord first, even if their friends haven't?

❑ In what ways can you provide ample strength for these valiant young men and women?

❑ How can you prepare your students for future days of discouragement or challenge?

❑ In what ways do you currently model this lifestyle for them, so that they are inspired to follow—even in the face of difficulty? What kind of memorable moments are you providing for them?

❑ What can you incorporate into your moments together to help bring about their desire to seek the Lord?

❑ What part does prayer play in seeking spiritual sensitivity and goodness? How does prayer help in seeking the Lord early?

❑ How have you helped your youth incorporate prayer as a way to seek the Lord early? In what ways would you like to improve this?

❑ What part does personal scripture study play in seeking the Lord early?

❑ How have you helped your students incorporate personal scripture study into their lives during your time with them? What can you do from this point forward to highlight this more?

❑ What part does serving others have in showing the Lord you are seeking Him?

❑ What other ideas come to mind in helping your students desire to seek the Lord early? Who can you have come as a special guest speaker to your class? Or is there someone the class could serve? What other ways could stimulate in your students a deeper understanding and desire to seek the Lord?

❑ In pondering these thoughts, what comes to mind as something you would like to try this week?

❑ The "measurables" of this goal are (time, place, how often, etc.):

Teaching by the Spirit
(Holy Ghost)

Which things also we speak, not in the words which man's wisdom teacheth, but which the Holy Ghost teacheth; comparing spiritual things with spiritual.
(1 Corinthians 2:13)

Corinth was an important town in the ancient Roman provinces. It also was a hotbed of split factions within the new Christian church. According to the "Bible Dictionary" in our King James version of the scriptures, Paul stayed in this community for a little under two years. He knew the individuals and the situation well. The writings he later sent to the Corinthians were not sent to proselyte, rather, they were sent to regulate. The early Church experienced obvious difficulties as it grew. The saints in Corinth not only struggled to understand certain facets of the gospel beyond the lens of familiar Judaism, they had other issues (see "Bible Dictionary," pp. 743-744).

The body of Corinthian saints mentioned in 1 Corinthians 2 are being rebuked for lack of unity, for impurity, for partisanship *and* insubordination. Ouch. Apparently, Paul still remembered these people well, having lived with them before the time of this letter.

Most of the Corinthian converts were Greek. The Greek people at that time were well-known for enjoying the pleasures of the body, and as such, were somewhat undisciplined and, at times, conceited. Yet the beauty of these saints is that they listened to their apostle! Word came to Paul that they had openly received his letter and had worked to remove impurity and insubordination from among themselves (ibid.). I'm sure he rejoiced for them.

What strikes me most from Paul's letter to these saints is his admonishment to instruct by the Spirit. To quote Paul, we are not to teach as "with enticing words of man's wisdom, but in demonstration of the Spirit and of power" (1 Corinthians 2:4). Paul works to show his learners the strength of God and the beauty that awaits the individual when they desire that the Holy Ghost teach through them, rather than rely on their own strength and knowledge. As teachers we can benefit from this instruction ourselves. Once we've grasped this, just think what it can do for our youth. They need to learn and experience instructing one another by the Spirit, also!

Joseph Smith taught, "And if any man among you be strong in the Spirit, let him take with him him that is weak, that he may be edified in all meekness, that he may become strong also" (D&C 84:106). Why is this the pattern given of God? The answer comes a few verses later, "...The body hath need of every member, that all may be edified together, that the system may be kept perfect" (D&C 84:110). This is our work and joy as gospel instructors and youth leaders—to offer edification to our students. Therefore, until all have become edified, our job is not done.

How do we bring this about, though, in a classroom or household of (at times) squirrelly teens? Our youth themselves experience lack of unity, as did the Corinthian saints at the time of Paul's letter. Our students may even be living lives of impurity or insubordination. A few students (which some might count already as "lost") may be like those ancient Greeks, relishing life after the natural man. Yet these concerns did not deter the apostle Paul. Not at all. In fact, it was precisely these kinds of issues which drove Paul to lengthen his stride, writing such powerful admonishments. His letter achieved amazing results! The saints cleaned up their lives. What an amazing sense of relief Paul must have felt. He then was able to turn his focus to other needs.

Our work, like the apostle Paul's, is urgent and continues on. Just when we think we've accomplished great things, another student may begin manifesting problems. But just like Paul, we continue to teach and model the things our students need to learn. One of those things is learning and teaching by the Spirit of God. Joseph Smith received this revelation to clarify misunderstandings about things of the Spirit.

> Wherefore, I the Lord ask you this question—unto what were ye ordained?
>
> To preach my gospel by the Spirit, even the Comforter which was sent forth to teach the truth....
>
> Verily I say unto you, he that is ordained of me and sent forth to preach the word of truth by the Comforter, in the Spirit of truth, doth he preach it by the Spirit of truth or some other way?
>
> And if it be by some other way it is not of God.
>
> And again, he that receiveth the word of truth, doth he receive it by the Spirit of truth or some other way?
>
> If it be some other way it is not of God.
>
> Therefore, why is it that ye cannot understand and know, that he that receiveth the word by the Spirit of truth receiveth it as it is preached by the Spirit of truth?
>
> Wherefore, he that preacheth and he that receiveth, understand one another, and both are edified and rejoice together. (D&C 50:13-14, 17-22)

Our youth need to experience the powerful uplift that comes into their lives when they learn and teach by the Spirit. To do this, they need to put off the "natural man" (1 Corinthians 2:14). When any of us live after the natural man, we are not as in tune to the things of the Spirit. Paul taught that this is so because the things of God appear "foolish" to those living after this manner. He also makes the point that spiritual things are "spiritually discerned" (ibid.). Thus it would be difficult in any measure for those living lascivious lifestyles to recognize, interpret correctly, and to value or embrace the things of God.

How essential it is then for our young men and women to purify themselves so they can receive the things of the Spirit whole-heartedly, spiritually discerning them as valuable and essential to a powerful life. Not only is this important for classroom activities, but it is essential for our youth in all environments, so that they may return to their Father.

Your Ideas

❑ For just a moment, close your eyes and imagine that the Spirit is present in great power in your classroom or at home. What brought it? How does it feel? How effortless is it to teach now? How are the students responding?

❑ In your own words, what constitutes teaching by the Spirit?

❑ In your own words, what constitutes learning by the Spirit?

❑ When a lesson is brought about by the Spirit, what kind of potency does it bring to both the student and the teacher? What happens to the relationship between all those involved?

❑ How do students benefit when lessons are taught after this manner?

❑ What might inspire a student to seek learning by the Spirit?

❑ What might inspire a student to seek to teach with the Spirit, rather than to rely on their own intellect?

❑ As teachers, what can we do to encourage this kind of atmosphere in our classrooms?

❑ What kind of accountability will we give when we appear before the Savior, if we have issues we never resolved that impacted our ability to learn and teach by the Spirit? How can you share this with your students?

❑ In pondering these thoughts, what do you feel the Lord would like you to do this week for your students or for yourself?

❑ What steps will you take this week to increase your own ability to learn and teach "by the Spirit," as Paul instructs us to do?

❑ In what ways can you make this goal measurable and achievable, with accountability?

Life's Instruction Book

(Scriptural Emphasis)

Let the word of Christ dwell in you richly in all wisdom; teaching, and admonishing one another in psalms and hymns and spiritual songs, singing with grace in your hearts to the Lord. (Colossians 3:16)

Whereas the Corinthian saints struggled with physical sin, the Colossian saints seemed attracted to internal sins—those of pride, intellect, and superior wisdom. In his letter to these saints, the apostle Paul taught of the danger of outward ceremonialism in lieu of reliance and union with the actual Christ ("Bible Dictionary," p. 746). Within the text of his Colossians letter, we have the beautiful admonishment of the above scripture, advising us to "let the word of Christ dwell in [us] richly in all wisdom."

As teachers and youth leaders, this is an essential task, to emphasize reading the word of Christ. We do not want our young men and women to look apathetically at their scriptures. Scriptures are the one actual "handbook" to life on earth given to us by the Lord. Our scriptures contain profound instructions on how to live joyfully and to avoid danger. Just as I'd hate to operate a "heavy-duty, double-bevel sliding compound miter saw" without first reading the instruction book, I'd hate to negotiate the complexities of life without the Lord's guidance.

Can a powerful 3,600 rpm saw really be any more dangerous than life in today's world? Yet people seem more willing to read a saw's instruction book than to read the Lord's instruction book.

In many ways, the world is not what it was when we grew up. The choices youth must make today come in dizzying speed and peril, mostly because of the technological advances which are upon us. Amidst this bewildering pace, scriptural counsel can make all the difference. For example, when a friend tells one of our youth, "It's impossible to find God in this world," our student can know the truth. They can respond, "God is not gone. In fact, He has promised, 'Draw near unto me and I will draw near unto you; seek me diligently and ye shall find me; ask, and ye shall receive; knock, and it shall be opened unto you' (D&C 88:63)." But our youth could only have this verse open to their minds if they are immersing themselves in the scriptures.

Knowledge of another verse could be helpful if a student's boyfriend were pressing her for physical relations. Whether or not she felt moved to share the following verse with him, she will have it to see her through to a wiser decision than she might make otherwise: "Prepare yourselves, and sanctify yourselves; yea, purify your hearts, and cleanse your hands and your feet before me, that I may make you clean; that I may testify unto your Father, and your God…that you are clean from the blood of this wicked generation" (D&C 88:74-75).

If students read their "handbook to life" on a consistent basis, they will *know* their scriptures, and those scriptures, in turn, can help them during perilous times. Living this way, they also will be far more likely to center their life on Christ, as Paul importuned his saints (and us) in his Colossians letter. As teachers, leaders and parents of these youth, we will not always be available to aid them. But as their gospel instructors, we can leave in their mind a legacy of love and value for the scriptures.

The Lord's handbook, that priceless compilation of prophetic utterances, means more to me than any other book I own. Today's youth can feel the same. They will achieve this by searching the scriptures, trying out the teachings for themselves. As they do this, Christ's words will prove themselves of worth and will dwell richly within them. A student reading from these pages just a few minutes a day and prayerfully pondering the message will find greater insights and peace than from any other source.

Our youth need to experience the fruits of gospel scholarship to value those fruits, to savor them, to use them. For in truth, can an individual become apathetic to the scriptures and remain faithful to the Lord over the years? It is highly unlikely. There is a power given us to dismiss sin when we daily read the Lord's word.

If we are not using the scriptures in our classrooms or our homes, what *are* we doing? Talking *about* the scriptures is not the same thing as *reading* them. We've discussed this before and it bears repeating. There is a difference, and our youth deserve the latter. Just imagine if you're the first gospel instructor in their life to take this seriously. The legacy you will leave your students will be immeasurable!

Students who are willing to walk privately on their own through the scriptural arbors of the Lord's fields of harvest are those students who do not faint under the heat of the world's sun. At some point a student must determine that they will rely on Christ's word and efforts, not the work, effort or words of another. Indeed, the point of spiritual success begins with a youth enthused enough about the gospel (or at least willing enough to trust), that they take of their personal time and use it in private gospel scholarship. These are the students who will reap dividends throughout their lives as they continue to study the word of the Lord in private sessions with Him.

The Colossian saints were admonished to let the word of Christ dwell richly within them. It is the same for us today. As a starting point, the Church as a whole has been asked to read the scriptures together in family units. As families, we are to discuss them and make application of their teachings, thus strengthening the family bond. But not all families do this. And no group scripture study can match the quiet hours when a soul seeks comfort, knowledge, or direction in private solace with the Lord and His sacred scriptures.

When are our youth going to learn the joy that private scholarship brings? Group study is one thing; private scripture study is something quite different. As we encourage our students to develop a habit of daily scripture study—through reading the scripture text for each current year of study—we give our youth a treasure which is immeasurable and which will enrich their lives for all their days on earth.

There is a noticeable difference in the youth who have struck out on their own into the lush green fields of the scriptures, who have made gospel truths and principles their own. The difference is clear; the fruits are strong and apparent in those young lives. Their hearts are full of the words of Christ; these are youth who can sing of the Lord's grace, rejoice in His strength, and walk back into His presence.

Your Ideas

❑ What kind of Spirit enters your life when you are not just surface reading the scriptures, but truly feasting upon them?

❑ What kind of Spirit remains with you, even when finished?

❑ Imagine two youth: one reads the scriptures, the other does not. Where are these two students at the end of the year? What impact has their study, or lack of it, had on them and the choices they have made?

❑ Why does the word of Christ have such an impact on your life when you study it consistently?

❑ Have you ever gone without reading the scriptures? What begins to happen? How hard is it to resume the habit of daily study? Why does this happen?

❑ What insight does this give you then to work with those students who are not yet reading their scriptures personally?

❑ In what ways can you get your students into the scriptures during your lessons? What ideas can you implement to give them consistent scriptural opportunities?

❑ What benefits can you demonstrate? Stories from your personal experiences?

❑ Some teachers have found ways to get their students reading without offering trinkets or candy as rewards. What are the benefits of this? What are some ways you can inspire your students to such an extent that scripture study becomes appealing without the enticements of trinkets? How can prayer help in finding ways to motivate scripture study?

❑ In pondering these thoughts, what is one thing you can do this year to increase your emphasis on daily, individual scripture study?

❑ List some other ideas or thoughts you have about getting your youth to read the scriptures, rather than just hear about them.

❑ How will you make your ideas measurable and achievable?

❑ How do you want to follow-up on your ideas?

❑ What would you like to incorporate this week specifically?

Milk or Meat?
(Scriptural Understanding)

I have fed you with milk, and not with meat: for hitherto ye were not able to bear it. (1 Corinthians 3:2)

R eading the scriptures is a good thing. Understanding them is even better. But for youth who have not consistently read their scriptures, the initial experience can be a little like tasting a new food. They recognize that others might like the taste, but it is still strange and foreign to them.

The saints in the ancient city of Corinth, like many of our youth, were new to the gospel. They struggled with the deeper things of the Spirit, because they were used to the easier things of the world. Paul tells them that they are carnal and that is why they experienced "envying, and strife, and divisions" (1 Corinthians 3:3)—all natural emotions and behaviors, coming easily compared to the more mature behaviors taught in gospel doctrine.

As our young men and women come in from the world, we can watch them experience a transfer of perspective. Whereas kids at the local high school may value pride, prestige, and wealth, with all the latest tech toys, the Spirit of God does not. Kids out in the world may enjoy crass jokes or attend irreverent movies—the Spirit does not tolerate such material. Each day our youth walk between these two worlds—that of the adversary and that of the Spirit. At some point, our young men and women will be making a choice of which one to inhabit permanently.

The scriptures will help our youth discern wisely between carnal lifestyles and eternal ones, but only if the scriptures are clear to them. If our students find the scriptures too deep to understand, this priceless handbook of inspiration remains out of reach—even if read daily. Youth grasp for truth, most seeking the good, but without knowing how to understand the message, their fingers will come up empty. The students will shut the scriptures and make an inaccurate assessment that whereas Christ's words are fine for their parents and teachers, they just don't seem to work for them. Paul recognized this immaturity amongst the saints at Corinth. He understood that they were yet as "babes in Christ" (1 Corinthians 3:1). As a result, he modified his teaching.

Do we want our students reading daily from the scriptures? Absolutely. Are they? For many of them, perhaps not. Why not? We need to follow Paul's example as we introduce the scriptures repeatedly throughout our time together. Each parent and gospel instructor has the responsibility to find out if a youth is or is not interested in their scriptures. We need to mold our lessons to our students' abilities, just as Paul molded his teachings to the Corinthians' current ability.

At the beginning of each year, we read verses together as a class and ask questions as to the important doctrines contained therein. Can our students deduce principles from what they just read? If they can't, this then defines our starting point as gospel instructors and leaders. We need to allow additional "play time" within the scriptures for the younger "milk" drinkers among us. Have you ever seen the children's sign, "My work is my play"? Well, for our youth, it can be the same. It truly can be fun to "play" in the scripture yard God has given us.

While exploring in this virtual/spiritual playground of enjoyment, we can show our students how to read not just for the story, but for the meaning behind the story. Remember the "5 Ws" our English teachers taught us? The "5 Ws" work well in spiritual environments as well! Some probing examples might be: "*What* brought these people to this point?", "*Why* do you think they were told this?", or "If you were there, *what* do you think Paul might have meant?" These are just a sampling of questions that can get youth exploring the principles waiting for them on the pages of their scriptures.

The more we have "playground time" in class, by using the scriptural blocks in the lesson material, the more our young men and women will grow in understanding the prophets, their messages, and their meaning. Our students may not yet be able to fully digest the "meat" of the gospel, but they sure will enjoy drinking the "milk." I trust the apostle Paul in his "milk" vs. "meat" approach. He knew what his learners could handle; he knew what would edify them. I also suspect that our youth are generally in a better spot than the Corinthians, making our job a bit easier.

I'm sure the apostle Paul arrived at his assessment through a variety of means; and how important that he did! By accurately assessing our students' understanding in a variety of ways, we can know how to share each lesson and just how much to let the students explore. By requiring their participation, we will strengthen them in their ability to understand what they read. As their comprehension grows, they really will be less and less like the Corinthian saints and much more able to understand and partake of the things of Christ.

Paul knew that those who live with envying and strife will struggle more with living the gospel than those who pursue Christ's pathway of peace. He also knew that contentious people struggle more with gospel doctrine. As gospel teachers, we can be gentle on ourselves as we seek to wean our students from the "milk" of Christ to the "meat." This can be a lengthy process. Our youth can only move as fast as they are willing to purify their lives. Until then, we offer the "milk" of the gospel to nourish them until they are able to receive more.

Incidentally, when Paul speaks of the "meat" of the gospel, I doubt he meant deep doctrines. In fact, his separate letter to the Colossian saints was in essence a reprimand for seeking after ethereal and complicated gospel topics. Rather, the gospel in its completeness is simply one of full-hearted faith, repentance, receiving ordinances, pursuing service, and enduring to the end. Not very complicated, but it requires a mature ability to live it. Thus, as we work with our youth, we need to understand that they are babes in gospel learning and application. It is true that, generally speaking, they no longer crawl in obedience to the many standards of the gospel, but at times their gait may be unsteady.

As our youth increase in mature obedience, their pace will become steady. They will be able to discern the Spirit and they will find strength in scripture study. This will happen, because their scriptures will begin to make sense to them. The words of Christ will become palatable, even desirable. This then is our job—to continually hold out the promise of joy for those who want to live the gospel in a "meaty" way. When the scriptures have become delicious to our students, they will be ready for that meat.

Your Ideas

❑ What do you savor most about scripture study?

❑ When was the last time you read your scriptures until completely saturated in the Spirit?

❑ Are there greater heights you can achieve in your scripture study? What feelings or gospel abilities will come as you do so?

❑ Why did the Lord give us the gift of scriptural nourishment and refreshment through the scriptures?

❑ What will it do for your students to be able to tap into the sweet inspiration of the Lord in this way? How will their lives be changed?

❑ What currently impedes your students from experiencing this?

❑ What do you feel impressed that you can do to encourage the transition from "milk" to "meat"?

❑ In pondering these thoughts, what do you feel the Lord would have you do this week to build your students' awe and love for the words of Christ?

❑ What brings hope that your students will understand their scriptures on a more mature level? That they will turn to their scriptures when confused or discouraged, rather than to something harmful? How can you model this for them throughout the year?

❑ What kind of classroom experiences do they need to increase their desire for gospel "meat"? What moments can you provide on a consistent basis so they can move from "milk"-based living to a "meat"-based life?

❑ Of all your students, which one concerns you the most? Whose face comes to you right now as needing the most help in this category? Write down their name.

❑ In thinking of him or her, their life, family situation, possible challenges, etc. (realizing much of this may be unknown), what might be this student's greatest, most silent heartache(s)? Jot down any impressions that come to mind.

❑ What could happen for this student to have the scriptures come alive for him or her?

❑ As you ponder this student, what can you add to your teachings this week to bring the scriptures to life for them and for the whole class?

❑ What are some specifics that can help bring this into focus, to help measure any improvement that might come? What do you see happening as a result of carrying out this goal?

❑ What will you specifically ask the Lord for this week to help your students discover the personal power of the scriptures?

The Flashlight of Understanding
(Wisdom)

And I have filled him with the spirit of God, in wisdom, and in understanding, and in knowledge, and in all manner of workmanship. (Exodus 31:3)

E xodus 31:3 perfectly describes the gospel teacher's call: to fill our students with wisdom, understanding and knowledge, thereby bringing the Spirit of God to their lives. Our young men and women are needed in this world. Just picture our youth living after this manner, the good they will bring to this world of trouble and darkness. Youth, full of the Spirit of God! Full of wisdom! Youth, full of understanding! Imagine the manner of "workmanship" made manifest through our students' lives lived in this way. This is our stewardship as parents, teachers and leaders—to do everything in our power to help bring this about for our youth. We teach it, they live it. But is this what really happens?

It could be, so easily. John Bytheway, in his *Standards Night* DVD, explains his experience that once kids *truly* grasp the principle behind a rule, they usually comply. It is a testament to the divine nature they carry within them. It is an amazing thing to watch happen. Sometimes just a little bit of understanding can do so much!

In fact, as adults, we are the same. If we can grasp the larger picture, smaller issues take their place much better within the scheme of the whole. When we grasp the "why," the *principle* of the thing, everything becomes easier in submitting our will to the will of the Father. This is otherwise called obedience, but some might simply call it love. When we can identify the principle behind a doctrine, our hearts can ensure our steadiness in following it. I've seen the beauty of this process at work in my own life.

Our youth will be better able to find their way through life if they can identify the eternal principles within the pages of their scriptures. These gospel principles become "flashlights" for life in this murky world; they light the way home. Our youth will be well-served when they can identify the doctrines and principles that reside behind the surface of the so-called rules we follow in the Church. To begin with, then, our youth need to learn this process by finding these same doctrines and principles in the scripture stories they know so well. When they can do this, they are much more likely to make obedient choices, because their minds and hearts will have been enlarged with the wisdom and understanding of the prophets, both ancient and modern. These young men and women will be much more likely to arrive safely home to God, bringing with them "all manner of workmanship" (Exodus 31:3).

The time is soon approaching when our teens will become adults and leave us. They must be able to pull out appropriate doctrine and principles from the scriptures they have in front of them. This will protect them and make them more able to deduce the wiles of the adversary. For example, even now they do not always hear sound advice from friends. They receive mixed messages on dating and appropriate physical behavior. What about the movie that was just released in theaters, but it isn't up to gospel standards? What other murky choices may face them—choices that on the surface may imply innocence, but more deeply imply rebellion against the very standards God has set through His prophets?

Some students might think to themselves, "Why does it matter? It's just a movie." But as John Bytheway so succinctly demonstrates, the ability to find the "why" behind the commandment has amazing power to save a child from a dangerous decision they might otherwise make. As gospel teachers, we need our students to dig deeper than surface understanding of the gospel. We need them to move beyond the rules and so-called "have-to"s in the Church. We want them to enlarge their spiritual resources so that gospel discipleship becomes attractive to them and integral to who they are and the choices they make. That is why we should consistently teach and renew the essential skill of principle and doctrine finding.

When our students can see our earthly experiences with the eyes the Lord has, we and they have achieved great things. Then they will be wise stewards of their body, their talents, and their time on this earth. This way, they will desire and actually use the "flashlights" the Lord has given them to see through the encroaching darkness of our times.

Where do our students find the brightest "flashlights," these light-giving and life-saving principles? They find them written on the pages of the scriptures, whose verses come alive when read by any tender soul seeking truth. These verses, contained in simple printed ink, live and breathe when touched by the desire of a person seeking truth. Isn't it amazing how the same passage might speak one truth to one individual, yet witness of a different principle to the next? Don't we want to shout glorious praises to the Author of our scriptures for such a personalized gift of vibrant life?

This is the power of the gospel of Jesus Christ and it is encapsulated in the pages of our scriptures. Our Lord infuses all His words with wisdom and inspiration. Scriptural verses are like self-guided spiritual missiles, propelling themselves to each reader's heart directly where needed with uniquely formed messages.

To fill our job as gospel teachers, we must not just teach the scripture stories found in the scriptures, but teach our students how to identify the doctrines and principles within these stories. This is nothing new to parents or gospel teachers; we have been admonished to do this for some time. If we do our job well, our students won't just see a bunch of archaic words. No, instead our students will see laid out before them clear and intelligible planks of doctrine. These planks will provide sure footing for our youth to walk upon, during their journey back to the Father. And these planks are visible, as Brother Bytheway teaches, because of the "flashlight" principles lighting their way. We must get these flashlights into our youths' hands!

How do we do this? By practice, practice, practice. Our youth must be given the space and time to practice searching for the principles and doctrines lining the scripture stories they know so well. The principles and doctrines are not that hard to find, but if we don't give class time for the "why" behind commandments, our students will not be blessed by them.

Thus, as parents, teachers and youth leaders, we provide research activities, questions, and group efforts to build this skill of understanding within our young men and women. As the youth increase in their ability to understand the true premises of Christ's gospel, they will be filled "with the spirit of God, in wisdom,…understanding,…knowledge" and good "workmanship," as the Lord told Moses long ago (Exodus 31:3). The "workmanship" from one such individual will be amazing; imagine the "workmanship" brought forth by an entire generation of youth!

Is it any wonder that their workmanship becomes remarkable? When you have a "flashlight" of understanding to see what you're doing, it's incredible what you can accomplish!

Your Ideas

❑ Are there any "rules" in the Church that your students seem to struggle with? If so, which ones?

❏ Can you find the guiding principles behind those rules? In other words, what might be the "why" behind the commandment or counsel?

❏ How can you help your students gain testimonies of living by the standards of the gospel? What are some ideas that come to mind that you could implement in the next few weeks?

❏ What does it do for a student to understand the underlying principle of the rules they struggle with?

❏ What does it do for a student to grasp the significance of the Atonement? How does this understanding affect obedience?

❏ Why might obedience (or lack thereof) signify the presence (or not) of an understanding of the Atonement?

❏ One of the most essential things we do when working with youth is to teach them to understand the gospel. But in reality, this might be better expressed as helping students to *find* and *understand* the principles behind each doctrine. What can you do to incorporate this into your lesson? If you were modeling this for a newer teacher, what would you do?

❏ As parents and teachers, why is it important that we ourselves are able to deduce the "why" or principle behind a commandment?

❏ Have you ever struggled with a commandment? If so, which one?

❏ What might be the underlying principle for this standard or commandment?

❏ How can you find out for sure?

❏ How did you (or can you) obtain a testimony of living that standard?

❏ It's painful to watch teens who are not wise-hearted in their choices. What can you do to bridge an understanding of the gospel into your students' hearts?

❏ What are you currently doing to ensure your students can find the principle "flashlights" after they leave your classroom?

❏ What works well in your current approach?

❏ What isn't working well?

❏ What would you like to modify?

❏ How can you make your plans measurable? In other words, how will you measurably incorporate your ideas expressed here into your teaching this week (time, date, specific activity, etc.)?

❏ Specifically, what will you do this week to ensure that your students are having the chance to practice identifying doctrines or principles in their scripture reading?

The Language of the Spirit

(Testify)

And after that you have obtained faith, and have seen...with your eyes, you shall testify..., by the power of God;...that I may bring about my righteous purposes unto the children of men in this work. (D&C 17:3–4)

In D&C 17:3–4, we receive an important teaching pattern: start in faith, obtain a witness, and then testify so that others might experience the ennobling process. Why? Because we are more than we think we are. God has a much greater plan for us than we know. Prophets have been allowed to pull back the veil just a fraction; what they've seen beyond our cloudy world stuns them in its beauty. All of it is waiting for God's children who seek Him, find Him, and then help others to do the same.

What a beautiful process! As we serve in the Church, there is such joy in witnessing the progression of mankind. Our Father is waiting patiently for all those who seek Him and His righteous purposes. How urgent it is that we join Him, to help Him in His endeavors. After we have obtained faith, we may seek a witness of our unseen God and His glorious intent. Once we receive our witness, the instinct is to share with others and to testify of the truths we've received. (To understand the essential nature of witnesses and of witnessing, read D&C 5:1-2, 15,

23, 32; 6:17, 22-24, 28; 20:13, 16; and Deut. 19:15. See Topical Guide, Witness, Witnesses.)

This process may be a new experience for our youth who are accustomed to a fast-food world. Remember the drive-in hamburger joint? You push a button, a voice is heard, you make your order, all without leaving your car! Everything is done for you. What a lopsided relationship. While it's nice when you need food fast, the rest of life does not happen in this way, especially with spiritual matters! With regard to spiritual events, it is a much more even relationship.

"And it is the Spirit that beareth witness, because the Spirit is truth" (1 John 5:6). This is one of the many roles of the Spirit—to witness of truth. The Spirit is the great testator and our youth need to learn that when the Spirit witnesses to them of a truth, the next step is for them to strengthen another by bearing witness of that experience to them. We read, "…And when thou art converted, strengthen thy brethren" (Luke 22:32). We do this to bless the lives of others (see D&C 18:15-16) and to avoid condemnation (see D&C 60:2).

This is not a new admonishment, solely for our time period. The Lord revealed to early covenant Israel, "Ye are my *witnesses*, saith the Lord, and my servant whom I have chosen: that ye may know and believe me, and understand that I am he: before me there was no God formed, neither shall there be after me" (Isaiah 43:10). The Lord wants us to know and believe; He wants us to understand that He is the one true God. Inherent within this privilege is the precept of being His witness. This process begins by receiving the initial witness brought by the Spirit; it is discharged when we recognize the experience and witness to another of it.

For our youth to testify and be witnesses, they need to know what it *feels* like when the Spirit is present. Can they identify it at this point in their lives? Identifying the Spirit of God goes beyond casual knowledge of the scriptures, "For the fruit of the Spirit is in all goodness and righteousness and truth;…the fruit of the Spirit is love, joy, peace, longsuffering, gentleness, goodness, faith" (Ephesians 5:9; Galatians 5:22) What does all this mean in practical matters to a fourteen-year-old ? As their teachers, we need to translate this into, "Remember the smile on your face last week when you helped Sister Martin down the hall? What kind of feelings were you having?" "Where do those feelings come from?" "It must have been great *to have felt the Spirit like that!*"

Another example might be, "Remember last month when you told me you weren't sure whether or not to go to Wyoming for the summer?" "Remember when you finally felt comfortable making the decision? What scripture was it that helped you?" "Oh, yes, that one. What feelings came that helped you decide?" "Oh, that is beautiful. Would you be willing to share that experience with our class tomorrow? I think it could really help them understand *what the Spirit feels like!*" Bingo. The light goes on. A connection is made on terms they understand.

That connection is essential because in the next five to ten years, our youth will be making some of the most important decisions of their young lives: where to go to school, what to study, whether to serve a mission, who to marry, *where* to marry. If they can't recognize the promptings of the Holy Ghost now, how will they successfully do so then? Will anyone step in, between then and now, to help them?

I don't want to run the risk that the youth I work with never learn the language of the Spirit. I don't think any teacher would. That's why, as leaders of youth, we give our students ample opportunities in class to learn to identify the Spirit and to testify of it. We help them understand the Spirit's presence, how to recognize it and how to respond. In fact, in many ways our lessons are simply beautiful vehicles to help drive these skills home.

Once a connection with the Spirit is made, joy comes naturally. But that connection is not our only goal. Once it is made, we need to give sufficient time for our youth to share what/how they felt, thus clarifying the experience and beginning to taste what it feels like to witness of it. Whether the sharing comes in the form of journal writing or verbalizing, it does not matter. What does matter is that sharing the experience is the next essential step in their growth as witnesses for the Lord. This doesn't need to take much time, but we need to be sure we provide the forum for our youth to do this! When they learn to step outside of themselves to testify of the Lord, His truths, and His love, not only have they lifted themselves, they've potentially brought another soul to God.

Our youth are missing out if they're not experiencing these great moments—both in and out of the class or home. When they begin to feel comfortable explaining, sharing, and testifying of what they know, there will be no stopping them. Not today's youth! Not with the potential they carry within.

How to get started? At the beginning of the new year, or in your first lesson with a new class, or even during your next family meeting, let the youth know that the Spirit will witness of truth as it is taught throughout the year. Invite the students to notice when they have felt the Spirit's warmth and light begin to flood their souls. Indicate to them that these are the moments to raise their hands and to share what they just felt. Do not stress that this must happen, only that doing so will strengthen others and themselves. It will draw all closer to the Lord.

Initially the students may feel a little awkward. They may need you to lead by example. When you've been listening to a class presentation, and you've felt the Spirit surge, you can raise your hand to share for just a moment what you've felt. None of this is meant to be contrived. On the contrary, you are simply alerting them that the Spirit will come as truth is taught. It is that simple. As sons and daughters of God, our youth have the privilege to feel the Holy Spirit and the opportunity and obligation to share it—either during the lesson or perhaps at the end when you turn the time over to the youth for any final thoughts, or in their personal journals.

As we seek the Spirit of the Lord, we will find it. It will grow within us as we improve our lives to receive it. Youth need to feel comfortable with the entire process; they will do so as we help them to recognize the

Spirit and then give them the time to explain, share and/or testify of what they are feeling. The more they do this, the more natural it will be for them to recognize the Spirit and to share with others.

Just as babies take months to learn to use their limbs in effective ways, students may take a while to learn to be comfortable with, and to speak about, gospel topics and truths. Depending on the maturity level, at first it can feel risky for a teen to be serious with their peers. They might feel awkward or vulnerable at first, but as they become more familiar with the Spirit, they are edified by it. Their ability to share the experience increases.

One would hope that all our youth receive this kind of spiritual nourishment in the home. But unfortunately, for some families, the only gospel teaching that comes is that found in the three-hour block of church on Sundays. Those called to a position to teach the youth have been asked to convey these important principles as a safety net, in case no one else does.

Thus, as powerful teachers, we want our students to have be skillful in sharing the gospel, fueled by a love of God and concern for their fellowmen. That is why we give them time in class to share and explain to each other, to ponder and to testify about verses or experiences that have gospel meaning to them. It might be rocky at first, but when we allow the students to take turns presenting portions of a lesson or to talk about what mattered most to them, they are learning to explain, share, and testify. They have this same opportunity when given an assignment to journal a moment in which they last felt the Spirit. They are experiencing a process that will bless their lives as long as they continue in it.

Far be it from me to want to be a blabbing monotone up at the front of class, burbling words that run one into another in a never-ending stream from an overflowing fountain. After a while, the desire comes to turn off the fountain and dry out. Instead, I want my students to be the ones to play, to splash, to get to know the delightful, refreshing waters of the gospel, the pure waters that come straight from Christ. Not knowing other factors in their lives, I must assume that my classroom might be their only opportunity to do this. Therefore I allow class time for it: the space necessary to explore the scriptures, to share what they have learned, and why it matters to them. It's one thing to hear your teacher talking about why the gospel is important; it's another thing to discover it for yourself. And isn't this why we teach? To bring these young men and women to the point of gospel enjoyment, scholarship, and strength?

There are so many ways to bring this to fruition. Whether it is assigning various groups to present their thoughts about a block of scripture, having the students write a script proving a principle's worth, or memorizing certain passages and then sharing the doctrine behind those passages, any of these events during class will stimulate our youth. They will be challenged to dig deeper to find the jewels at the bottom of the fountain of Christ's living waters.

When our students grasp these principles and make them a part of their lives, these precious youth will change in spontaneous ways because the truths have begun to matter to them. Harmful habits, unkind ways of speaking, unhealthy choices will be left behind. Our youth will stand on a path of pure beauty built from gospel study and stewardship. As they practice explaining, sharing, and testifying, they will walk more firmly upon that path. They will no longer be infants in Christ, but maturing sons and daughters of God who please the One who created them.

Not only will our youth be comfortable explaining the gospel to each other in class, they will find themselves easily sharing and testifying of saving truths to others outside of class. They have now increased their faith and received their witness. "And after that you have obtained faith, and have seen…with your eyes, you shall testify…, by the power of God;…that I may bring about my righteous purposes unto the children of men in this work" (D&C 17:3). As a result they can instinctively testify of God with power.

Your Ideas

❑ What are your personal feelings about the gospel? If your great-grandchildren were with you right now, what would you share?

❑ Share an experience where you undeniably felt the Spirit.

❑ What does it do for youth to understand the Spirit on this level?

❑ As teachers we give class time to the students so that they may share, explain, and testify. What is the difference between these three different approaches?

❑ Do you feel you currently allow sufficient time to assess your students' understanding of these three different modes of missionary work? Have you allowed time for them to explore these principles by sharing with each other in class? If so, what have you done that has worked well? What hasn't worked well? How can you modify this for greater impact?

❑ Why are students shortchanged when teachers do all the testifying in class?

❑ What is the benefit to a student to have the opportunity to share their feelings about the gospel with their peers in class, even if it is awkward at first?

❑ What ideas have come to you that you can implement in your lessons?

❑ What can you do to ensure that these moments do not feel forced?

❑ We testify of things in many ways—not just at the pulpit. How can you stimulate discussion on what testifying means? Is it just through our words that we testify? Can it be something more? What about our actions, do they add to our verbal witness? Ask your students these questions and record some of their thoughts here.

❑ How can we, as adults, avoid a 'holier-than-thou' attitude when it comes to teaching these matters? In other words, how will you help your youth to feel they are included in this process of learning the language of the Spirit, rather than feeling like their experiences are less important or less spiritual than yours?

❑ The area needing focus most in your class would be (select one):

- Learning how to share doctrines and principles of the gospel
- Learning to articulate/explain clearly those doctrines and principles.
- Learning how to testify of experiences/witnesses brought by the Spirit.
- This particular group of students needs help learning to do all three.

❑ In pondering these thoughts, what ideas has the Lord brought to your mind?

❑ How can you make these ideas specific and attainable for your class?

❑ How will you measure your follow-through to ensure you do not forget your ideas?

❑ In thinking about your students, what will you do this week?

Perfectly Portable Scriptures

(Scripture Mastery)

Ye shall the know the truth, and the truth shall make you free.
(John 8:32)

L et's stop for a moment and take a breather, reviewing a few important concepts. Successful gospel teachers seem to follow a fairly similar path. Their journey begins with learning by, then teaching by, the Spirit. The second leg of the journey comes when they have the aptitude to allow the same for their students. They creatively encourage their students to read their scriptures on a daily basis, then ascertain whether their students understand what they're reading. If so, great! They move their students towards the "meat" of the gospel, teaching the youth how to find eternal principles and doctrine within those scriptures. If not, these teachers take the time to help the students become familiar with the scriptures and how to get the most from them.

This takes a lot of effort. Even if we already do these things, we can set goals and implement them for better classroom moments. We do this, because the process strengthens the youth. But this is not the end.

I believe our purpose is far more global than just getting our students to a point of gospel scholarship. Life is not just about *our* one or two or twenty young men and women. Once our youth understand the gospel (because they're reading and living it), it becomes urgent for them to move their sights to the next level of discipleship, that of explaining, sharing, and testifying to others of the Lord's gospel truths (which we discussed in the previous chapter).

These truths exist not only to set our students free from the darkness of this life; they exist to set all of God's children free. But so many of them are still unaware. Why? "For there are many yet on the earth among all sects, parties, and denominations, who are blinded by the subtle craftiness of men... and who are only kept from the truth because they know not where to find it" (D&C 123:12)

The truths of the gospel—if lived—keep God's children free: free from sin's clutches, from unnecessary sorrow, and from needless pain. John recorded Christ's promise, "And ye shall know the truth, and the truth shall make you free" (John 8:32). Do we not want this enacted on behalf of everyone on this planet? Well then, who is going to do the work of sharing? It falls to those of us who already have the truth. *This* is the larger picture to which we must raise our sights. And if we need a reward for doing the labor, that's all right. "He who does God's work, gets God's pay," or so the expression goes. That pay, according to the prophets, is marvelous. I want my students to be the beneficiaries of that eternal paycheck.

How will I bring my students to this next level? I will arm my youth with some of the most potent "sharing, explaining, and testifying" tools that exist for God's workers: nuggets of scriptural text that seminary kids call "scripture mastery." In these small pieces of truth abide potency of the most magnificent kind—additional "flashlights" of truth to light our way. When our youth not only understand these doctrinal "flashlights," but also have them committed to memory, they are ready to light the way for anyone who might need assistance, at a moment's notice.

These nuggets are not just for seminary; they are available to all who are willing to make use of their potency. Yet I wonder how many members in the Church avail themselves of these amazing nuggets of truth? Just twenty-five verses to be learned each year, for a total of 100 doctrinal tools just waiting to be put to work. What compelling power awaits those who do!

The world is full of people seeking truth and who do not know where to find it. Having a mental container full of bite-sized scripture nuggets makes sharing, testifying, and explaining so much easier for our youth (and ourselves). When our young men and women reach a level of comfort in discussing these things with their church peers, then they are ready to open up their horizons. How much more comfortable will a youth be when speaking with someone at school or even with an adult if they have such doctrine at their immediate command?

No wonder seminary students are asked not just to memorize these scripture mastery verses, but also to be able to find them in their scriptures and to explain their significance. This process does so much for our youth. By working daily to memorize them, they are focusing on priceless truths. The deeper the memorization, the deeper the potency and impact of the verse for that young life. Know the truth, be set free in so many ways. Free to deduce Satan's wiles. Free to receive greater joy while in this life. And especially free and ready to share the gospel with others.

These tools are not to be used to "Bible bash." Far from it. Hopefully our youth would reject such contentious discussions, seeing "Bible bashing" for what it is—foolish and full of ugly pride. No. These priceless nuggets are simply reserved for those who are troubled and seeking greater light and knowledge. A scripture mastery verse from any of the four standard works can be so helpful to a youth who understands it. When they have memorized it, they stand ready at a moment's notice to aid a lost soul, whether in a class at school, on a ride at Disney World, or in any other place.

For example, while walking with a friend at the beach, the friend might share with our student a feeling of powerlessness in their life, that they are starting to succumb to temptation. They want help but don't know who to turn to. Our youth, with an ever-ready supply of scriptural nuggets, can reach out and touch that honest person's heart. This particular scripture mastery verse might come to mind: "Wherefore, men are free according to the flesh; and all things are given them which are expedient unto man. And they are free to choose liberty and eternal life, through the great Mediator of all men, or to choose captivity and death, according to the captivity and power of the devil; for he seeketh that all men might be miserable like unto himself" (2 Nephi 2:27). They can then explain that these feelings come from the adversary and that the Savior can help dispel them.

In a flash, our student can help their friend with the words of God, which are intended to break through darkness, ease confusion, and bring balm to a troubled soul. All simply because this youth took the time to memorize his scripture mastery verses.

Memorizing key scriptural passages helps our kids know how to reach out to those who are seeking or who are confused. The Lord has promised that His sheep will hear His voice, recognize it, and desire to follow it. The scriptures contain His voice. When our youth stand ready to share with their friends or other acquaintances, the result can be the following: "And they all cried with one voice, saying: Yea, we believe all the words which thou has spoken unto us; and also, we know of their surety and truth, because of the Spirit of the Lord Omnipotent, which has wrought a mighty change in us, or in our hearts, that we have no more disposition to do evil, but to do good continually" (Mosiah 5:2).

Imagine our youth being part of such a process and knowing they had prepared themselves to do so! What a life-changing and testimony-strengthening event. Scripture mastery is not just for the memorization process alone, although that has great benefit. It brings so much more. As parents, teachers and leaders of youth, we can inspire these young men and women with the greater view of its significance and power. We as a people speak so freely about emergency preparedness for natural and manmade disasters. What about spiritual preparedness for emotional disasters? I cannot tell you how convenient it has been that I could share a scripture with another during a sudden and difficult moment—even though my actual scriptures were at home!

Our youth never know when a need will arise for them to explain, share, or testify of God's truths. They may not have their physical scriptures with them "24/7," but these essential 100 scriptural "packets" can travel with our youth wherever they may be. This concept of always being ready to help the Lord's lost can be a large part of that urgent vision we mentioned at the beginning of the chapter—the vision that we are not just here to save ourselves, but to offer that salvation to others. The Lord has decreed that those who don't share will stand condemned (D&C 60:2). How aware are our students of this responsibility? How prepared are they? Let us do what we can to support them in this, especially by helping them with these 100 nuggets of truth. By learning them, our young men and women stand ready at a moment's notice to help another with the saving balm of the scriptures. By energizing our youth about the power of scripture mastery, we give them the gift of perfectly portable scriptures.

We can revive our love of this essential part of teaching and support our youth by asking how their scripture mastery memorization is going. Together, all of us can open their eyes to the possibilities that stretch ahead of them because of their diligence in memorizing these potent scriptural gems.

We know God's children are out there, lost and confused, not knowing the direction home. "For there are many yet on the earth among all sects, parties, and denominations...who are only kept from the truth because they know not where to find it" (D&C 123:12). Do we turn a blind eye on these individuals in our midst? What a powerful moment of realization for our students when they realize that all the hours spent in scripture mastery pursuits can lead them to one (or more) joyous moments of sharing, explaining, and testifying to a questioning soul. How great will be our students' wonder as they experience the gospel through their friend's eyes for the first time. By knowing these key scriptural passages, our young men and women will more easily be able to share, explain or testify of specific gospel truths. These truths will set the hearts of their friends free. How great will be their joy as they share the potential of eternity with their friend.

Truly this can be a higher purpose for scripture mastery activities, rather than just winning an award or prize at the end of the year. The layers of purpose are many. Elder L. Tom Perry has said, "Just as a building is constructed one brick at a time, the Savior's true Church is built one conversion, one testimony, one baptism at a time" (*Ensign*, May 2005, p. 87). Our students can participate in this, especially if they have made these bite-sized scripture nuggets a part of themselves.

Your Ideas

❑ Why do you feel the that youth have been asked to memorize the 100 Scripture Mastery verses?

❑ What does it do for youth to participate in this?

❑ Do you feel your students have captured the vision of what memorizing these passages can do for them? If not, what are some ways you could bring a broader purpose for scripture mastery to your class? How can you help this come alive for them?

❑ What could ruin the joy of scripture mastery for your students?

❑ What can you do to help make sure this does not happen?

❑ How do we as teachers make sure our students understand that "Bible bashing" is devoid of the Spirit?

❑ How many of the scripture mastery verses have you memorized?

❑ How many can you still quote?

❑ How can you help your students avoid getting locked into "perfectionism" with scripture recitation, as opposed to the overall Spirit of the purpose?

❑ What type of classroom activities do you use, or do you plan to use, to extend the scriptures into practical applications? In other words, it's one thing to recite a scripture perfectly, but it's another to actually understand it and be able to apply it to life's experiences. What are some of the ideas you plan to use to help your students move to this deeper level of understanding and application?

❑ What are the benefits of a teacher memorizing these verses along with his or her students?

❑ In thinking of your students, are there any who struggle with memorizing and have given up? If so, who are they?

❑ Rather than leaving them to struggle on their own, what are some things you can do to nurture them in this important work?

❑ In pondering these thoughts, what do you feel the Lord would have you do this week for your students?

❑ How can you make this specific and measurable, so that it is achievable?

100 SCRIPTURE MASTERY VERSES

OLD TESTAMENT	NEW TESTAMENT	BOOK OF MORMON	DOCTRINE & COVENANTS
Moses 1:39	Matt. 5:14-16	1 Ne. 3:7	JS–H 1:15-20
Moses 7:18	Matt. 6:24	1 Ne. 19:23	D&C 1:37-38
Abr. 3:22-23	Matt. 16:15-19	2 Ne. 2:25	D&C 8:2-3
Gen. 1:26-27	Matt. 25:40	2 Ne. 2:27	D&C 10:5
Gen. 39:9	Luke 24:36-39	2 Ne. 9:28-29	D&C 14:7
Ex. 20:3-17	John 3:5	2 Ne. 28:7-9	D&C 18:10, 15-16
Ex. 33:11	John 7:17	2 Ne. 32:3	D&C 19:16-19
Lev. 19:18	John 10:16	2 Ne. 32:8-9	D&C 25:12
Deut. 7:3-4	John 14:15	Jacob 2:18-19	D&C 58:26-27
Joshua 1:8	John 17:3	Mosiah 2:17	D&C 58:42-43
Joshua 24:15	Acts 7:55-56	Mosiah 3:19	D&C 59:9-10
1 Sam. 16:7	Romans 1:16	Mosiah 4:30	D&C 64:9-11
Job 19:25-26	1 Cor. 10:13	Alma 32:21	D&C 64:23
Psalm 24:3-4	1 Cor. 15:20-22	Alma 34:32-34	D&C 76:22-24
Proverbs 3:5-6	1 Cor. 15:29	Alma 37:6-7	D&C 82:3
Isa. 1:18	1 Cor. 15:40-42	Alma 37:35	D&C 82:10
Isa. 29:13-14	Eph. 4:11-14	Alma 41:10	D&C 84:33-39
Isa. 53:3-5	2 Thes. 2:1-3	Hel. 5:12	D&C 88:123-24
Isa. 55:8-9	2 Tim. 3:1-5	3 Ne. 11:29	D&C 89:18-21
Jer. 16:16	2 Tim. 3:16-17	3 Ne. 27:27	D&C 121:34-36
Ezek. 37:15-17	Heb. 5:4	Ether 12:6	D&C 130:18-19
Dan. 2:44-45	James 1:5-6	Ether 12:27	D&C 130:20-21
Amos 3:7	James 2:17-18	Moro. 7:16-17	D&C 130:22-23
Mal. 3:8-10	Rev. 14:6-7	Moro. 7:45	D&C 131:1-4
Mal. 4:5-6	Rev. 20:12-13	Moro. 10:4-5	D&C 137:7-10

Teach Plain Doctrine
(Clarity)

*Come ye near unto me; I have not spoken in secret; from the
beginning, from the time that it was declared have I spoken;
and the Lord God, and his Spirit, hath sent me.*
(1 Nephi 20:16)

T he Lord does not work in the dark. He makes His expectations
known. His standards are no secret; His desires for our progress
are clear. His efforts, warnings, and admonishments are delin-
eated in the scriptures and are reiterated time and again by our
modern-day prophets. The Lord wants to make sure we "get it," for
there can only be one chance at this earth life. He desires that we have
joy during it and succeed at it. He has done all things possible to make
that available to us. He has repeatedly shown how to receive exaltation,
if we will but hearken.

This is the pattern we follow as His teachers, youth leaders and
parents. We issue the clarion call; we set the standard. We want our
students to live a life of joy, rather than experience the heartache
spoken of by Isaiah, "O that thou hadst hearkened to my commandments! then had thy peace been as a river, and thy righteousness as the
waves of the sea...There is no peace, saith the Lord, unto the wicked"
(Isaiah 48:18, 22).

The Lord expects us, as His servants, to teach His gospel and nothing but. Our expectation is that the students will listen and apply it. We teach plain doctrine so our students will know to avoid the pain that travels the stealthy path of rebellion. We want them to avoid the pernicious sorrow that lines selfish matters. We want them to know the One to whom they can look for pure comfort, guidance and truth. This is why we center our teachings around Christ—nothing more and nothing less.

That is why we are told to be so careful in what we include in our lesson materials. Our time is so short with these young men and women. We are to focus on the pure truths of the gospel, as found in the scriptures and taught by modern-day prophets, not some commentary we purchased from an LDS bookstore. Much like Isaiah, who continually circled his lessons around the need for righteous reliance on the Lord, we too join with the holy prophets by centering our lessons on core spiritual truths given us from the Lord. In so doing, we hope to bring our students to redemption at the feet of the Savior.

To make a difference, we must choose wisely how we use each minute during our lessons. We must teach so that our youth have a solid understanding of the restored gospel. This forms the bedrock of who we are as Latter-day Saints. It encompasses what we believe. The restored gospel of Jesus Christ is a crucial part of every lesson we prepare, whether on the plan of salvation, the Atonement, or any other tenet of our faith.

Teaching with such clarity and concentrated purpose does not mean we cannot be upbeat. On the contrary, the gospel message is one of uplift and yes, even joy. We do not need to be boring; it is not a sin to laugh while working with our youth. But when those lessons are delivered, we want to stand approved before the Lord. We do that by ensuring we have taught the core components of the restored gospel in each and every lesson we teach. I don't want to waste their time, nor mine, nor do I want to have to explain to the Lord why I got lazy in some of my lessons. The Judgment Day is always present in my mind. I am very aware that every moment in front of my students is being recorded by some celestial "cam" and one day may be viewed as part of my stewardship review before the Lord.

I think you must be pretty much the same, or you would not be reading this book. We want our young men and women to be able to clearly articulate the plan of salvation, truths about the apostasy, and the need for a restoration. We especially want them to comprehend the magnificence of the Atonement and what the Savior has done for them.

These things are not new, but how easy it is at times to drift from them in our lessons. Yet we must not. We must not let one lesson pass us by without referencing the magnificence of God's plan for us in some way. For isn't that what this is all about, being teachers for the Master? We are to be about the business of preaching the actual gospel of Jesus Christ, based on the scriptures and church-approved materials, rather than filling our lesson times with cute stories and motivational thoughts. We are not working to become "motivational speakers." We are called to be gospel teachers and we are asked to do so with great clarity and power.

Call me intense, but the day will come when each of us will be required to give an account of the time we spent with our youth. There is balance in all things, but did we do what we could for our youth? Was it enough? Or did we simply fill their itching ears with plentiful tales that led nowhere in general, other than to entertain (2 Timothy 4:3). Perhaps this is too demanding for some gospel teachers, who would rather let the days slip by easily and without too much trouble. But when each day with our students holds so much potential, why choose to live to a lesser level?

Joseph Smith was a model of such fervor. Listen to his words!

> Brethren, shall we not go on in so great a cause? Go
> forward and not backward. Courage, brethren; and on,

on to the victory! Let your hearts rejoice, and be exceedingly glad. Let the earth break forth into singing....

Behold, the great day of the Lord is at hand; and who
can abide the day of his coming, and who can stand
when he appeareth? For he is like a refiner's fire, and like
fuller's soap; and he shall sit as a refiner and purifier of
silver, and he shall purify the sons of Levi, and purge
them as gold and silver, that they may offer unto the
Lord an offering in righteousness. Let us, therefore, as a
church and a people, and as Latter-day Saints, offer unto
the Lord an offering in righteousness; and let us present
in his holy temple, when it is finished, a book containing
the records of our dead, which shall be worthy of all
acceptation (D&C 128:22, 24).

There is much work to be done and these youth of ours will play an
important role in it. Yet the world that these youth face is treacherous;
choices are flung at them faster and harder than in any age past. Thus
we need our students to have a solid grasp on why they are here, where
they came from, and where they are going—which is essentially the
great plan of salvation encapsulated.

When we teach plain doctrine, we will have students who will
follow—because they will have felt the surge of the Spirit testify boldly
that this is indeed the gospel of Jesus Christ, authorized by Him. Then,
as Isaiah points out, our young men and women will be far more likely
to choose a life of peace like "a river" and righteousness as "the waves
of the sea" (Isaiah 48:18).

The Lord makes His "secrets known" (see 1 Nephi 20:16) through
His prophets, thus making these blessings possible. He teaches with
great clarity; let us do the same.

Your Ideas

☐ Why are we asked to teach core doctrines, rather than cute stories, in our class time with our students?

☐ What does it do for a youth to be knowledgeable of such integral gospel doctrines as the plan of redemption and of the Atonement?

☐ What are some activities you could do to assess your students' understanding of these basic tenets of our faith?

☐ In pondering about your students, who are you most concerned about? Do they have a grasp on the significance of why the Lord created the plan of redemption? What does this mean to this particular student? And if this understanding is missing, what can you do to remedy this?

☐ What are some activities you could do to illustrate the significance of the apostasy?

☐ Why is an understanding of the apostasy so crucial to understanding the restoration of the gospel?

☐ What is one activity that would illustrate the restoration and its importance to our lives today?

☐ In thinking back on the apostasy and its deep impact on the world, what are some activities you could use to help your students share the message of the restoration? What lessons from the manual might fit this best?

☐ We often say that the Church of Jesus Christ of Latter-day Saints is the only true church. Considering that a definition of "true" is "rightful, legitimate, the true heir," how could this definition help you teach your class why we say this?

☐ To be "living" means to possess or exhibit life. How is it that our church can be described as "living"? What part does the priesthood play in that?

☐ When thinking about the grandeur of the restored gospel and that which the Lord gives you through it, what amazes you most?

❑ What efforts do you feel you could incorporate into your lessons this week to increase your students' core knowledge of the gospel?

❑ How can you make these measurable, so that you'll more likely achieve them?

His Hand Is Stretched Out Still
(The Troubled Ones)

And the arm of the Lord shall be revealed; and the day cometh that they who will not hear the voice of the Lord, neither the voice of his servants, neither give heed to the words of the prophets and apostles, shall be cut off from among the people. (D&C 1:14)

Whatever do we do with the student who actually refuses to hear? When it seems that everything we've tried meets with deaf ears and an unfeeling heart? When they refuse to abide by class standards and make things difficult for everyone around them? Do we invite them to leave?

It depends.

We must ask ourselves, "Does the Lord ever give up on His children?" The answers are mixed in the scriptures. Isaiah speaks forlornly about the children of Israel, "Therefore, is the anger of the Lord kindled against his people, and he hath stretched forth his hand against them, and hath smitten them; and the hills did tremble, and their carcasses were torn in the midst of the streets. *For all this his anger is not turned away, but his hand is stretched out still*" (2 Nephi 15:25; emphasis added).

The Lord, through His prophets, has also said, "O house of Israel, is my hand shortened at all that it cannot redeem, or have I no power to deliver?" (2 Nephi 7:2) We also read, "O ye fair ones, how could ye have departed from the ways of the Lord! O ye fair ones, how could ye have rejected that Jesus, who stood with open arms to receive you! Behold, if ye had not done this, ye would not have fallen..." (Mormon 6:17). Again from Mormon, "And when they had sworn by all that had been forbidden them by our Lord and Savior Jesus Christ, that they would go up unto their enemies to battle, and avenge themselves of the blood of their brethren, behold the voice of the Lord came unto me, saying: Vengeance is mine, and I will repay; and because this people repented not after I had delivered them, behold, they shall be cut off from the face of the earth" (Mormon 3:14).

Apparently there comes a time when the Lord will stand back and allow His people to destroy themselves. He will not intervene. Yet during that time, His hand is consistently stretched forth, ever eager for the repentant soul to grab. It is for this moment Christ lives. He was crucified for this purpose, so that all souls who turn to Him may be rescued and redeemed.

The Lord allows His children choice—to follow Him or to defiantly oppose His work. He allows them the individuality of making their paths and walking in them. But forever he stretches forth His hand, to save them if they turn to Him.

As parents, teachers and youth leaders, we need to follow the steps of the Master. First, we need to make clear our standards and hold firm to them. For example, we let our students know there is a decorum of modesty and of respect that is required (not requested) of the Lord's youth. Attendance is a privilege.

So might there come a time when tough choices must be made, if the student refuses to abide by classroom standards? Perhaps. Classroom standards are meant to be maintained, not bent or broken for a student simply because they don't feel like living them. The decision should be something worked out in counsel with the student, his or her parents, the bishop, the auxiliary president, and the Lord. Yet, as long as the student is willing to work, to try to lift himself or herself to a high standard, we remain firmly with the Lord—hands continually extended.

The gospel is for all of God's children. Let us not be like Jonah, who wanted to select which cities and which people *he* thought should be given Christ's message (Jonah 1–4). No, as gospel instructors we are called to preach to all of our students, even the slow-of-heart. As long as they will abide by the standards needed to maintain a classroom full of the Spirit, we will embrace their presence in our classroom.

In summary, our job is to teach, not to handpick *who* we want to teach. We keep our hand stretched out, ever reaching, just like the Master. Our students choose whether or not they will take it. We pray they will.

Your Ideas

❑ Do you currently have a troubled student who fits this scenario?

❑ If so, how have you tried to reach him or her?

❑ Have you counseled with the bishop, parents, and auxiliary president regarding this youth? If so, what suggestions did they have?

❑ How much time have you spent in consistent prayer regarding this situation? Have you fasted for this student, either on your own or with others?

❑ Have you attended any of this youth's extra-curricular activities (if there are any)? For example, basketball games, choir concerts, etc.

❑ Have you met individually with the youth to express love and interest in their well-being, to explain classroom standards, and to problem-solve with them?

❑ Bring this student's face to mind. What impressions come as to what might be their greatest challenge or heartache in life?

❑ Brainstorm a bit and write down at least ten ideas of how you can serve this youth.

❏ Which idea would you like to incorporate this week?

❏ How can you make these action plans measurable and specific?

Standard–Bearing Youth

(Righteousness)

And I saw the dead, small and great, stand before God; and the books were opened; and another book was opened, which is the book of life: and the dead were judged out of those things which were written in the books, according to their works. (Revelation 20:12)

We stand firm for our youth. They are making such valiant choices just coming to class. On top of that, there are youth who actually follow the standards written in the "For the Strength of Youth" pamphlet. These youth in particular deserve ample sustenance from our lessons. Unfortunately, rather than being celebrated by their friends, sometimes they are rejected—by their church-going peers!

I've seen it happen all too often. Their friends from church want to live "in the world," which leaves the standard-bearing kids outside of the "clique" in the ward, during a time when social life means so much. It can be lonely for a teen who wants to live correct standards, especially if the majority of their church peers couldn't care less.

The concept of the gospel is *supposed* to go like this, "Now therefore ye are no more strangers and foreigners, but fellow citizens with the saints, and of the household of God" (Ephesians 2:19). Guess what. That isn't happening in certain groups of the church, where teens are ridiculed if they don't follow their church friends into certain movie theaters, dances, or clubs. It often comes down to this: want a large social group? Then be willing to do whatever the crowd wants. This, even amongst the youth in the church! It may not ever be talked about, but it is happening and is apparent to perceptive leaders on the sidelines. Paul described this when he talked about the last days and individuals who were "despisers of those that are good" (2 Timothy 3:3). Who knew that those despisers would be kids from church!

I suppose that this should not come as too much of a shock. We can read of the same problem among the Nephites, "Now it came to pass that there were many of the rising generation that…did not believe the tradition of their fathers…and their hearts were hardened" (Mosiah 26:1, 3). Among this group of hard-hearted youth were the sons of King Mosiah and the son of Alma the prophet. These were wicked and idolatrous young men who created much heartache among the members of the church. Although we do not usually find a situation this extreme within our wards, we do at times see covert ridicule and unkindness from certain youth towards the others who quietly refuse to bend their standards.

How sad this is. How disappointing that standard-bearing youth would have need to relate with those who followed Enoch during a time of huge wickedness. These individuals "confessed they were strangers and pilgrims on the earth" (D&C 45:13). Righteousness can bring loneliness, if but for a time. As teachers and youth leaders, we need to be aware if this is happening in our classroom.

Our young men or women who choose to live the gospel deserve all the love, support, and inspiration in our lessons we can muster for them. They may have walked out of a friend's party, because of the movie being shown, thereby losing a friendship. They may refuse to cheat with the rest of the class during a math exam, thereby gaining quiet honor, but loud ridicule. They may refuse to dress with their belly button showing or their pants drooping, thus earning the ridicule or disdain of their peers.

These youth are fighting battles we may not know. Now that they have arrived in gospel citizenship, which initially might have felt like a foreign land, these youth deserve to be treated as the victorious pilgrims they are. They need all the love and assurance we can extend them. Whether it's our friendly smile, eyes of concern, or the strong hand-shake welcoming them to class, these kids need this kind of support. We do not know what forces may have sought to pull them down just the night before. Nor can we know the inner anguish they carry or the sacrifices they have made to be with us. But to quote President Thomas S. Monson, "The decision to change one's life and come unto Christ is, perhaps, the most important decision of mortality" (*Ensign*, May 1997, p. 44). Let's celebrate the youth who have made this choice and encourage the rest to follow!

Your Ideas

- ❑ Ponder for just a moment the students in your class. What kinds of interaction, both subtle and not so subtle, do you observe?

- ❑ Have there been any interactions between students that have concerned you? If so, what were they?

- ❑ Which students worry you the most?

- ❑ What perspective might the Lord have of these interactions? Take a moment to jot down the thoughts that come. How might you best support the youth who are trying to live the standards of the gospel?

- ❑ How might you best help those who have not yet "jumped on board" to gospel living?

- ❑ What might influence these youth?

- ❑ Are there any factors that you feel could be discussed with the bishop, from a leadership perspective, to help these youth?

❑ In considering possible approaches to help or support our youth who *do* try, what are possible negative repercussions of these approaches? In other words, what could make it worse for the students?

❑ What would the Lord have you do this week?

❑ How can you make this measurable and achievable?

Appendix

A Year at a Glance

And it came to pass that I, Nephi, said unto my father: I will go and do the things which the Lord hath commanded, for I know that the Lord giveth no commandments unto the children of men, save he shall prepare a way for them that they may accomplish the thing which he commandeth them.
(1 Nephi 3:7)

You are to be commended for all you do to serve the Lord and His youth. Use the pages found in this appendix to record your accomplishments and those of your youth! Whether it was that you chose to speak calmly while frustrated with a student or that your students all accomplished a class goal for the month, these pages are to help you celebrate these exciting events. Make copies of these pages and put them in your teacher's journal or planning book. Then simply take a little time at the end of each week, while setting the next week's goals, to record these happy gains in your classroom. Dive in at the month you are currently in and begin celebrating!

MONTHLY GOALS

Divide the three goals you chose on page 38 into twelve monthly goals. Make two copies of this chart. Write each of the monthly goals in a square. Put these charts in your planning calendar. Write the goals on individual note cards and tape them on your bathroom mirror to help you remember.

GOAL 1	GOAL 2	GOAL 3

MONTH: _____

Each week, there were exciting breakthroughs! They were…

WEEK 1	
WEEK 2	
WEEK 3	
WEEK 4	

The overall cause for celebration this month was…

MY TEACHER'S STATEMENT

My greatest desires for my students are:

_____

_____

_____

_____

_____

_____

I feel the purpose of my call is to:

_____

_____

_____

_____

_____

Three of my greatest abilities are:

_____

_____

_____

_____

_____

When our time is finished as a class, my students will be grateful for me because we specifically:

_____

_____

_____

_____

_____

_____

When I appear before the Savior, I will present to Him my following efforts in behalf of this class:

_____

_____

_____

_____

_____

_____

MONTH: _____

GOAL SHEET AND MEASUREMENT TOOL

My overall goal for this month is to:

_____

_____

_____

_____

_____

In reviewing this book and the notes in my teaching journal, I'd like to incorporate the following area of focus into this month's lessons:

_____

_____

_____

_____

_____

_____

In breaking that emphasis into smaller, measurable pieces, I will focus on a different angle each week.

Week 1, I will model:

_____

_____

_____

_____

Week 2, we as a class will:

_____

_____

_____

_____

Week 3, we as a class will:

_____

_____

_____

_____

Week 4, the students will:

_____

_____

_____

_____

At the end of the month, I will be able to measure our success by:

_____

_____

_____

_____

_____

_____

WEEKLY PLANNING SHEET

Date:_____

PRE-WEEK PLANNING
What I intend to accomplish this week:

_____

_____

_____

_____

How I intend to do this (listing minutes used, activities led, students involved, etc.)

_____

_____

_____

_____

_____

_____

_____

_____

_____

_____

_____

_____

POST-WEEK PLANNING

Of all the things I used in class, this worked the best this time:

_____

_____

_____

I think it was because:

_____

_____

_____

This did not work as well:

_____

_____

_____

Perhaps because:

_____

_____

_____

Overall comments and recommendations for next week's efforts:

_____

_____

_____

_____

_____

About the Author

C.S. Bezas graduated from BYU in communications, with an emphasis in developing training and educational programs. She also took seminary teacher development classes while studying at BYU. She now teaches early-morning seminary in the southeastern portion of the United States. Additionally, she has conducted trainings for audiences both large and small on a wide variety of topics, appearing both as a keynote speaker and workshop facilitator.

C.S. Bezas has won recognition for her writings and stage musicals and has performed before audiences on television, stage, and film, most recently appearing as Anne Frank with the Florida Orchestra in the historic Mahaffey Theater. She writes a regular column for Meridian Magazine and is the creator of a new series of soothing therapy music CDs, the first of which debuted in 2005 and can be found at http://csbezas.com. She is pursuing her degree in health and is hard at work on her next book, *Powerhouse Health: The Word of Wisdom Made Easy.* C.S. Bezas and her husband have four children and relish the gospel of Jesus Christ.

Interested in having C.S. Bezas speak to your group? Whether for a regional youth fireside, Stake Enrichment meeting, workshop, or singles conference, she has spoken on a variety of topics and delights the participants with her insights and abilities to inspire. For more information, write to *info@powerfultipsforpowerfulteachers.com* and receive a free complete Teacher's Journal PDF file.

What People Are Saying

Powerful Tips for Powerful Teachers is more than a guide for teaching youth. [These] gospel-centered thoughts are a treasure trove for adults hoping to build faith in teens. C.S. Bezas' tips and ideas will warm your heart while strengthening your resolve to be part of preparing the next generation.
    —David G. Woolley, Ph.D. in Organizational Behavior, author of the Promised Land series

The youth of the church are engaged in a daily battle for their spiritual freedom. We stand beside them with the ammunition they need to fight the adversary: the gospel of Jesus Christ. Sister Bezas teaches us that when we are given great responsibility, great blessings await. Throughout this book she gives us gentle reminders of the Lord's promise to teachers as we accept the responsibilities—and blessings—of teaching the youth.
            —Patricia Wiles, member of SCBWI, author of the Kevin Kirk Chronicles

Your creativity is such a blessing to all us teachers who wrack our brains every day to keep our kids awake, interested, and inspired to study the scriptures on their own. Thank you!
    —Trina Boice, author of *Sabbath Solutions, Easy Enrichment Ideas,* and *Climbing Family Trees*

As an early morning seminary teacher and a mother, I am so grateful for the principles taught in *Powerful Tips For Powerful Teachers.* I love plain speaking and plans of action. This book contains both, along with encouragement and hope. I had never thought of the importance of recording goals and keeping a record of class activities and impressions. I am grateful for helping suggestions about how to implement these success principles into my teaching, both in the classroom and at home. What a valuable tool!
                    —Barbara Packard, New Port Richey, FL

Powerful Tips for Powerful Teachers is solid spiritual pedagog. Anyone who works with young people, whether a beginner or a veteran, will find this book useful. Cindy Bezas' principled theory is aimed directly at the spiritual needs of today's youth. Using scripture as text, prayer as lecture, and journal as workshop, this book prepares parents, teachers, and youth leaders for the most important role they'll ever play....This is the book every youth leader needs to read.
    —Willard B. Gardner, M.S. in English, author of *Race Against Time* and *Pursuit of Justice*

What a trip! Reading *Powerful Tips for Powerful Teachers* really captures... much of the experience of the early morning seminary teacher. It has been many years since I taught a seminary class, but reading this book took me down memory lane. Sister Bezas will help the beginning teacher anticipate some of the very real challenges of early morning seminary and experienced teachers will also benefit from her suggested tools to overcome these challenges. The author has performed yet another service to mankind in writing this book. Thank you!
                —Dr. Gary McCallister, Ph.D., Professor, and composer of *Mormon Blues*

Also from C.S. Bezas

A Time for Ana

Soothing piano solos that calm and relax. Great for listening to while you read the scriptures or prepare lesson plans.

Available at most LDS bookstores or at www.rosehavenpublishing.com

Additional Titles by C.S. Bezas
Coming in 2007

Powerhouse Health: The Word of Wisdom Made Easy

How to beat fatigue and find reservoirs of increased energy by following the Word of Wisdom.

Power Tips, Volume 1

Tips, games and lesson plans for parents and teachers of LDS youth.

Sunrise (CD)

Another fabulous collection of piano solos to ease your heart and enrich your soul.